DATE DUE

# Nationalism and Ideology

## Books by Barbara Ward

BARBARA WARD

Jackson, Barbara (Ward)...

# Nationalism

## AND

# Ideology

*The Plaunt Lectures, Carleton University, Ottawa*

W · W · NORTON & COMPANY · INC · New York

In Memoriam
Adlai Stevenson

# Contents

# Nationalism and Ideology

## Chapter One

# The Return of
# Nationalism

TODAY we need above everything flexibility and the ability to move. This does not mean any question of giving up principle or faith, but simply that in a period of change and of vastly accelerated scientific development, we must be prepared to adapt our institutions, re-think our philosophies, and be ready with fresh ideas and fresh thoughts about old truths and habits. Nowhere is clear thinking more necessary than in the fields where our habits and thoughts have their deepest, most unconscious roots. And perhaps of all our communal habits none is more profoundly anchored than our national sense.

In a way this is surprising. Many of us came out of the last war with the feeling that nationalism, as the most violent force in world society, was to some extent in retreat. In the Western world a certain revulsion had taken place against the whole idea of the nation-state as the overriding center of loyalty. The unspeakable crimes committed in the name of National-socialism gave us the feeling of a whole community afflicted by a paranoidal breakdown. What good could there be in a feeling capable of such abuse? To this was added memory of the Great Depression and the long years during which the whole industrialized Western world seemed to be wallowing in purposeless incompetence. The conclusion was not difficult to reach that the nation-state offered no solution to Europe and was incapable of providing a rational framework for its acute economic and social dilemmas. Those who felt this revulsion against brute nationalism found their views enormously reinforced by the success of the Marshall Plan, which far transcended local, national interests and brought people together to solve their problems in a wholly new way.

And so for ten or fifteen years after the war, the feeling in the Western world that nationalism was no longer the dominant political philosophy was fairly strong and secure. But now we are beginning to realize that nationalism has a lot of life in it still. The feelings in which nationalism is rooted and to which it can appeal are by no means dead. A revived Western Europe, a decline in Soviet belligerency, Chinese resurgence—all these changes in the world balance of power have changed emotions and reactions too. We may not yet know how general this revival is. Nor do we know whether it reaches out to a new generation. But we do know that some voices are now raised to talk once again in terms of absolute loyalty to the primacy of the nation-state.

The Eastern bloc of Communist states has gone through something of the same cycle. There, too, the belief was current after the war that nationalism had been left behind. Nationalism in Marxist terms was simply a reflection of bourgeois groups manipulating the nation for their market interests. Impose control on Eastern Europe in the name of the superior world philosophy of Communism and the states would forget their separate, national origins and their rival, national interests and merge in one great Soviet Socialist brotherhood with their powerful neighbor to the East.

Yet if we look back over the last ten years, the most noticeable fact in Eastern Europe has been the revival of a sense of national community in Hungary, Czechoslovakia, in Poland, to a lesser degree in Bulgaria, and above all, perhaps, in Rumania. These nations have not abandoned Communism but apparently they do not intend to allow appeals based on "Communist solidarity" to contravene national interest and *they* will define where that interest lies.

In addition, the Communist bloc seems to be nurturing an even tougher form of rivalry. Between Russia and China there are signs of the oldest and most violent form of nationalist dispute—an absolute slap-up, ding-dong, flat-out frontier quarrel. In Central Asia over the last two hundred years, large stretches of bleak desert, steppe, and mountain have been removed from areas claimed by the Chinese for their sphere of influence and transferred to Russian imperial control under the tsars. We seem to live today in the age of the liquidation of empires. Yet it is possible that these two old empires may be in the process of reviving the oldest and most violent of disputes, a dispute about national frontiers. Thus behind the whole magnificent superstructure of world brotherhood, there is a nagging little return to the old nationalist approach. East or West, it makes no difference. What we thought was no longer the strongest force in the world is showing signs of a serious comeback. It seems to be overcoming what we might call bourgeois supranationalism in the West and Communist internationalism in the East.

If we do indeed face a revival of the old nationalism, we can judge it today by only one criterion: Will it contribute to human survival? Our times are much too precarious to allow us any luxuries in our political approach. What we have to do is to weigh the single question—whether this method of organizing human affairs will or will not lead to the extinction of the human race. Once we are extinct, it will not much matter how perfect, how platonic, how dialectic, how Marxist, or how anything else our politics were on the way to annihilation. There will then be nothing but an empty star spinning through space. Survival is thus the only context within which we can look at the claims and pretensions of any political movement in the world today.

( 14 )

The context has added urgency, for whatever the ideology—nationalism, socialism, communism, internationalism—we are living through a particularly precarious phase in human affairs. Again and again in human history certain moments recur that carry with them a special danger to peace. When one system of political order and control begins to break down, the problem of the rearrangement and realignment of power in some new system becomes acute and normally violent. All through history these moments of disintegration in political structure, followed by the emergence of new forms of pressure, have been, in Professor Toynbee's phrase, "times of troubles." The old power has ebbed, the new power is not yet clear. Meanwhile, uncertainty gives an extra edge of fear to the relations between states struggling to achieve some new stability.

Today we are going through such a phase on a scale the world has never seen before. We are witnessing all round the world the disappearance of Western colonial control. This control, if we look at it collectively, created the largest single imperial system in man's history. We do not yet know what is going to take its place. The world's power relationships are all being either subtly or brutally changed. We cannot rely on any status quo and every change is doubled with the risk that it may lead, by way of declining solidarity, less understanding, and further divisions between communities, to the ultimate catastrophe of nuclear annihilation. This is the only relevant context in which to look at the problems raised by nationalism and ideology.

⬤⬤⬤⬤⬤⬤⬤⬤⬤⬤⬤⬤⬤⬤⬤⬤⬤⬤⬤⬤⬤⬤⬤⬤⬤⬤⬤⬤⬤⬤⬤⬤⬤⬤⬤⬤⬤⬤⬤⬤⬤⬤⬤⬤⬤⬤⬤⬤⬤⬤⬤⬤

⬤⬤⬤⬤⬤⬤⬤⬤⬤⬤⬤⬤⬤⬤⬤⬤⬤⬤⬤⬤⬤⬤⬤⬤⬤⬤⬤⬤⬤⬤⬤⬤⬤⬤⬤⬤⬤⬤⬤⬤⬤⬤⬤⬤⬤⬤⬤⬤⬤⬤⬤⬤

## Chapter Two

# The Community

WHAT kind of problems in human relations do these two movements, these two principles of social organization, try to solve? Clearly, they were not just casually invented. They serve profound social and political purposes which, in turn, are rooted in a fundamental characteristic of human nature. Man cannot be alone. He cannot work alone. In fact, he has no possibility of being fully human unless he lives in a community. He is born into a family because of his overwhelming need for years of protection and training. And the moment life on this planet became more elaborate and passed beyond isolated families engaged in hunting and fishing, communities with more than a simple relationship of kinship began to form. The tribe is already a collection of families, and like every other later and more complicated community, required various forces to hold it together. And I would like to suggest that if we look back over the history of mankind, three factors constantly recur in the formation and preservation of communities.

The first is the sense of belonging to *this* particular group, community, or state and not to any other. It is a kinship in space and usually a kinship through time. What this kinship will consist of—once you get away from the simplest links of blood or parentage—depends very much on the second factor, the way in which people explain the world to themselves.

With the coming of consciousness comes the beginning of questions, above all the ultimate question: "Why is man here; what is the purpose of the community; what is the meaning of life itself?" It is, I think, significant that many of the very earliest remains of man tend to be burial sites and graves. Human beings, save in utter collapse and crisis, do not fling out their dead to lie and be picked to the bone. They have always felt that something about man demands that the significance of his death should be registered. And this is also an attempt to make some statement about the meaning of his life. This need for significance is at the basis of all attempts to explain the universe and man's part in it; and the kind of explanation in turn profoundly affects the type of ties and bonds which men create in their community.

The third element—the ways in which men organize

the work and the economic resources on which they depend for food and survival—is closely related to the other two. In fact, one of the most audacious attempts ever made to produce a unified and hence a supposedly "scientific" explanation of man's existence subordinates all other elements to this underlying structure of "productive relations." The Marxist progression of human development from the communal, propertyless tribe through the slavery of the archaic empires, the modified servility of feudalism, the wage-slavery of capitalism, on to the final return to communism at the highest technological level, the whole process propelled forward by the actions and reactions aroused by unequal property relations, has the magnificent sweep of a great epic. It also contains insights which have altered forever the way in which men look at history. But of course it is not science and it is not history, since it neither explains nor even includes all the facts. The elements of kinship, ideology, and work interact upon each other in every phase. But each has its own autonomy, and the infinite richness and variety of human communities follows from their myriad and unpredictable coalitions.

If we now go back into history to look at different kinds of institutions and societies, we are not leaving the modern world. We are not even leaving the post-War world. If we could look at our world society as a sort of showcase of societies, it might remind us of a museum devoted to the evolutionary development of species from the dinosaur to Homo sapiens—but in this museum all the types are still alive, all are still functioning. Tribal societies of enormous antiquity are still active and vigorous today. Communities with their roots in the millennia of the great world religions have survived, old empires taking the form of new states. And when we come to nationalism—which is one of the very latest of the formulations of man's kinship, man's meaning, and man's work—we find the new nation-state coexisting, as it were, with all manner of societies which go back over the whole span of human evolution.

The child in the womb recapitulates the whole phase of evolution. In our own world society today nearly all the phases of social and political evolution are still present. We have in New Guinea hundreds of villages each with a separate language. We have in Africa states so small—Mauretania, Gabon—that they have not got the population of a medium-sized American city. And China at the other end of the scale includes a quarter of the human race. These vast disproportions make all generalizations about policies and needs in our world society extremely precarious. They make decisions which have to cover more than one state—and most do—extraordinarily difficult even to formulate. How do you reconcile interests which spring from conditions so radically different? How do you even aim at order and concurrence and joint action in so incurably various a world?

When, therefore, we plunge back in time to look at the forces holding together man's experiments in community, we are not going back to what is now extinct. We are looking at the coexistence of various species of society—even though we may feel that some of them are reaching the outer rim of extinction. We may, for instance, surmise that tribal society, having vanished in the West and in large parts of Asia, is approaching its term. But this possibility does not counteract its present vitality. We cannot, for instance, understand anything about the Congo crisis—or, for that matter, the Nigerian crisis—without some grasp of the problems of cohesion, of regional competition between kinship groups, of traditional hostilities between tribes, which take us from the surface frictions of ideology and politics to an underlying, inherited, and tribal reality. The earlier forms are not distant; in space today we have what are in fact immense coexistences of time. Men at the first phase of political organization have to confront and work with men from the very latest. All this adds immense confusion to the task of policy-making. But the facts and difficulties must be known, for there are few quick answers and not many short cuts. Meanwhile, the larger issues of peace and war may depend upon good understanding.

# Chapter Three

# Tribalism

HOW DO the three themes —of kinship, of ideology, of function—find expression in tribal society today? And tribal society is, of course, the point where we all started. The surprise felt by European travelers in Africa in the nineteenth century is no different from Spanish Arab reactions to their crude Merovingian neighbors in the ninth century or the Romans' first appraisal of the ancient Britons and Gauls. They all found crudities and simplicities which they had left behind. But they had all passed over the same road.

On our experience so far, we could argue that tribal society is the most stable form of human society ever evolved. Certainly it has lasted longer than any other—

probably a hundred thousand years, possibly more; we simply do not know. Against this immense longevity, it is strange to set the fact that we in this century may be the last generation able to observe tribalism as a living system. Tribalism in its present form has no possibility of survival beyond this century. What we see in Africa, today, is its death throes as the loyalties, ideas, and technology of more elaborate societies sweep over it and erode the ancient landmarks. This is not to say that the death throes will be quick. Institutions with such a weight of history behind them fight stubborn rearguard actions. (It is not impossible that the nation-state is similarly doomed and similarly recalcitrant.)

In tribal society the sense of kinship is still above all linked to the family, to blood relationships. The tribe is usually composed of a number of clans, kinship groups, and extended families. But all have the sense of deriving their community from the same common ancestors and of handing on land, traditions, and sacred places to common descendants. There is an immense feeling of biological continuity and family solidarity, of knowing who you are and who your neighbors are, or better still, of not caring, because you are all one. This tribal unity is probably the closest unity the human race has ever known, and behind some of the extremer forms of nationalism today there is a harking back, a hankering at the very root of the psyche for that sense of being comfortably and exclusively with one's own kindred which is the norm in tribal society. Equally, the dark side of this cosy familiarity is rejection of the alien and the stranger and hatred of unaccustomed people and things. The early hominids dug up by Dr. Leakey in Kenya already have stones buried with them which are sharpened into weapons to keep out the stranger. Man is no different today.

The kinship of the tribe is also held together by particular explanations of the meaning of life. These beliefs have immense variety because the societies themselves have immense variety. We can hardly expect the same outlook among yam-diggers as among caribou-hunters. Some changes spring inevitably from different functions. Nevertheless there are also common insights made by man into his social condition which we find in his first articulated society—the tribal society—whether it is in the Congo or West Africa or Polynesia or among the North American tribes. On closer examination, we can still find these same strands in society today.

Clearly, primitive man felt himself to be surrounded by mysteries and powers over which he had no control. It was only, it seems, slowly by imitating nature that he learnt such vital victories over pure chance as the sowing of seeds or the herding of cattle and goats. We call tribal religion "animist" because it is full of spirits—of water and fire and forest and mountain, of the tribe, of its ancestors. But "power" would be as accurate a word as "spirit." For our world *is* full of power. We have pushed back the limits of mystery until we can study the stars that were extinguished before man reached his first tribal state. But the inconceivable energy which sustains a host of solar systems remains as mysterious to us as a flood or an earthquake seemed to tribal man. And some of our ways of dealing with the unfathomable facts of existence resemble his.

He sought security and reassurance in the close unity and continuity of the tribe. His ancestors were protective guardians, the customs of the group safeguards of right and propitiatory behavior. The encircling darkness of unpredictability and fear could be thrust back a little in the company of his own kind. Modern man protects himself in much the same way even if the units are larger. He even personifies his tribe in archetypal figures—John Bull, Uncle Sam. There may be a hint of the totem in Russian bear and Chinese dragon. To love one's own helps to cast out fear. Unhappily it can also entail as keen a hatred for the outsider.

Even where we seem most remote from tribal attempts to explain the meaning of things—as in the use of magic—the gap is perhaps not so great as we think. In a sense magic is primitive man's technology. We use technology to get us what we want. Since it is based on hundreds of years of scientific experiment, it works magnificently in many fields. It will take us to the moon. It staves off death. It controls floods and increases the harvest. Tribal man had only the beginnings of experimental technique—some knowledge of herbs, acute observation of animal behavior as an aid to hunting and taming, objective criteria to judge seasons and places favorable to good harvests. For the rest, he had to rely on the only controllable energy he knew—his own will power, or if you like, wish fulfillment. Since the human will, purposefully directed, can have a remarkable impact, particularly on other wills, some results of the focused will of the witch doctor could be and can be remarkable—especially since they were probably chosen from among men and women of particular psychic gifts—second sight, hypnotism, and so forth.

In our day, technology has reduced the role of magic to those fields in which no known technology is available. But there magic goes on. You have only to pick up any magazine and see what cold creams and cosmetics will promise women to know that magic is fully practiced to this day. Lightly disguised as wish fulfillment, it is very profitable. Much more money is made out of it now than was ever made by witch doctors in the past. They do not exactly give us love-philters but by the time you have read what Mr. X's perfume will do for you, it seems as near a love-philter as makes no difference. The need to control events—which is at the root of magic—is as strong as ever. But technology does so much controlling that magic slips back to the areas still obstinately obdurate to all our skills—love and destiny and fate and death.

Yet magic—the sense of powers or spirits present in all phenomena—and the protective authority of the tribe do not exhaust primitive man's desire for explanation. Again and again—from the dark forests of North America to the sounding surf of the Barrier Reef—we find a further, shadowy, ill-defined but constantly recurrent sense that behind all the smaller spirits, there is an ultimate source of power and being—a sky god, a great father, the ground of being, the first cause. Even at the time of his greatest physical isolation and most meager grasp on physical reality, man seems to have groped for a universal explanation which would confront his actual experience of tribal separateness with the possibility of wider loyalties and a greater state.

Yet tribal man's methods of production underlined both the close unity of the tribe and the exclusion of the outsider. In tribal society to this day, the land belongs to the community and is vested in the chief. He allots certain areas to individual families, but it is not "theirs" except for use. Many of the capital works—clearing, village building, path laying—are communal. Men help with each other's harvests. Each family produces for subsistence with a little barter on the side. The system looks inward, knows few differences of wealth, and owns almost no property. All this reinforces a single, dense, interconnected sense of communal life.

Once hunting ceases to be the main source of food, the land is the only source of subsistence. If its fertility fails, the tribe dies. This explains the importance in African agriculture of the long fallow. A family will need about twenty acres of land but only four acres are used at a time and the family moves round in about a twenty year cycle, the virgin bush springing up again once the soil enters on its fifteen year rest. There is no other way of restoring fertility and the cycle has given Africa a very extensive pattern of farming. Where land is available—and over much of Africa this has been the case— the long fallow and shifting cultivation preserve the soil and give a stable base to tribal farming. But if drought sets in or population cuts down the fallowing time, the tribe must move or starve. And when it moves, it soon strikes other tribes' lands or hunting grounds and wars for living space in the strictest sense begin.

Yet it is a stable society. It has lasted at least a hundred thousand years and is still vividly alive in Africa today. Many of the roots of African life are still deeply embedded in the close pattern of tribal relationships which have immense stability and can give very great human satisfaction. But each element of cohesion is now under strain. A single tribe is too small to carry the weight and satisfy the pretensions of modern politics. Animist religion retreats before technological change. A poor stable type of farming cannot withstand the desire for more opportunity and greater wealth. Tribalism in its strict sense is probably in the last decades of its organized, effective, public life. Yet it lasted so long and remained so unchangingly stable that we may well wonder how mankind ever broke out of this comfortable, reassuring, but basically static tribal trap.

Chapter Four

# An Age of Empires

THE BREAK comes with the rise of the great empires. At this stage, the pace of history seems to begin to accelerate. After the hundred millennia or more of tribal society, we move into a period of more rapid and precise change. The dominance of great empires in the world, each based on a separate but universalist philosophy, lasted only some three or four millennia. Although three of these empires—China, India, and Russia; two ancient, one fairly modern—may have made the transition to the contemporary world by becoming "nation-states" on a monstrous scale—one more reminder that the past is also contemporary—it looks as though this phase, too, of human history has reached its term.

( 28 )

How did it begin? One possible explanation is that in certain river valleys—the Yellow River, the Euphrates, the Nile above all—the skills needed to control water and develop effective irrigation for farming were so much beyond the tribal groups' organizational and administrative capacity that urgent technical need helped to set up a more elaborate society.

In Egypt this change seems to have been brought about by a wave of dessication which came over the Mediterranean. The choice lay between learning to control and use the water of the great river—or starvation. Some of the tribes of Egypt retreated before the drought and moved south into the deep swamps of the Sudd. Today, the Dinkas and the Shilluks of the Sudan, who are fighting a rearguard action against control by the Arab north, may well be the direct descendants of this retreat.

The first great civilization of man was built by those who stayed behind and began to measure and control the Nile. As the river rose and fell, harvests and sowings had to be arranged in due season. Fields had to be prepared and measured so that the inundation did not wipe out the pattern. Such measurements required geometry and trigonometry; magic began to recede before the theodolite. And all this observing, measuring, and calculating, coupled with the scale of organization needed to put the calculations into practice, began to affect the whole fabric of cohesion—new loyalties, new explanations, new techniques had to be found to underpin a new kind of society.

Another and more brutal engine of change—from tri-

bal times down to our own—has, of course, been conquest. Once a large and successful tribe has absorbed
other, weaker groups, the need to discover new forms
of cohesion is inescapable. History is strewn with em-
bryo empires that never quite achieved the unity needed
for survival, and like the successive empires of Mali and
Ghana and Songhai along the southern borders of the
Sahara, arose and flourished under a great leader and
then declined as incompetence at the center and im-
patience or rapacity on the fringes broke the unity up
again. None of these empires lasted more than three
hundred years. But then the West's colonial empire has
not lasted any longer.

In some areas, however, conquest extended the scale
and consolidated the power of systems which were
stable and continuous enough to become centers of
new civilizations. China, Northern India, Mesopotamia,
Egypt—all these by internal change and external conquest created a new range of social organization at
about the same time and with some strong features in
common. In this "age of empires," kinship, ideology, and
function take on new forms.

First of all, cohesion—natural, unforced cohesion—is
much less. We have left the almost biological unity of
the tribe behind and now we meet a series of rather
precarious arrangements of power which may in fact
explain why so many lesser empires were short-lived.
Conquest is the immediate cause of empire but cannot
preserve it. Otherwise the Assyrians or the Mongols
would have left behind the most coherent of social

( 30 )

orders, whereas in fact they have sunk from history almost without trace. It is only by transcending conquest that the conquerors could create new systems and set mankind on a new path. Yet the very scale and elaboration of a larger society made cohesion more difficult both at the top and the base of society—at the top because the incorporation of lesser chiefs and lesser rulers in a wider order surrounded the central power with jealous, defeated, and pretentious men; at the bottom, because distance, administration, the elaboration of new functions and new offices separated the rulers from the ruled, opened up new gulfs of wealth and self-interest, and turned the old propertyless tribal unity into a long and complicated hierarchy of more or less privileged people.

Of the two, the danger from disaffected subordinates at the top was always the greater—for they could on occasion in times of deep stress rally a disaffected province against the central power. Normally the farmers and laborers at the bottom confined their loyalty and their influence to the village and left the dynasts to carry on their squabbles at the highest level. But wherever the new conqueror had to leave essential power, including military power, with his conquered vassals, any lasting unity was beyond his grasp. It seems that the ease of Cortez's incredible conquest of the Aztec empire lay in the discontent and disaffection of Montezuma's vassals on the coast. The vigor of feudal life in Western Europe helped to defeat all efforts of either pope or emperor to establish continental unity.

Only where the dynast had direct centralizing instruments of power did coherent imperial states arise. Often the instrument was the non-regional army—Rome's legions, Turkey's janissaries, the army of the Hapsburg empire of which it was said "Austria itself is in your camp."

Sometimes the instruments were administrative. The great dynasties of Northern India—the Mauryas, the Guptas—were underpinned by an administrative structure which took the dynast's rule directly into the provinces. The Moghuls established a system of civil service rule through local collectors which the British copied and adapted. But it is to China that we must look for the supreme example of continuity through direct administration.

Three or four centuries before Christ, China was riven with feudal struggles. The old mythical unitary rule of the "Yellow Emperor" had given place to cutthroat war. At this point, the victorious dukes of Chi'in, having knocked out the competing feudalities, established a new central authority.

Then under the Han dynasty, Confucius' mild and worldly wisdom was made the philosophy of state—a point to which we must return—and in place of the old feudal administrations, the emperors set up a centralized civil service of mandarins. These mandarins became the controlling element of a unified society. They mediated between the head of the dynasty and the mass of the people and could do so more easily because they were chosen very widely from among the people, and were recruited on the basis of real skill and real intelligence. They were even chosen by competitive examination about a thousand years before the British introduced the system. They were also appointed to serve in provinces away from their relatives—a move which in a family-dominated society assured their disinterestedness. It was, above all, this continuous administrative machine, sharing a common culture and ideals and dedicated to centralized power, that has given China over two thousand years of coherent existence and carried down to the modern world a state structure established in the heroic age of empires when dinosaur states arose on the remnants of a fragmented tribalism.

Now we must come back to Confucianism. At this point, kinship and ideology fused to paper over the cracks of conquest and privilege. In most of the great empires, the dynast is made the center of the philosophy designed to explain to the people the meaning of their society and their place in it. The little gods and totems of animist religion are absorbed into a universal religion in which they join a hierarchy of divinity. At the head is the god of the ruling dynasty and the dynast is either his high priest, or in a symbolical sense, his presence on earth. All that art and architecture can do to enhance the divinity of the dynast bursts forth in vast temples and overpowering monuments which ring the world with ruins as gigantic as the dead empires that raised them up. All this magnificence is part of the attempt to raise men's loyalties above the local group and to incorporate them into a living relationship with the dynasty. Divine attributes are given to the king, since he must remain the center of loyalty and the center of meaning for a society which might otherwise founder back into the old fragments.

Even in China, this concentration of power and philosophy is a potent force of cohesion: "even" because China was in many ways the least religious of all the great empires, the most down-to-earth, the most worldly. Confucius would have made an admirable guide for British gentlemen—he has such good taste, such *savoir faire*, such a sense of the possible and the permissible. Yet this same Confucius also preached the visionary doctrine that the whole goodness of the empire was sustained by the virtue of the emperor. The empire's great public act of union was the annual dedication by the emperor of the whole "Middle Kingdom" to the Way of Heaven. Thus the emperor became the ultimate source of meaning for society as a whole, and the identification of the people with the dynast was cemented by the belief that his virtue was their fate.

Yet it would be wrong to see only the cement of a new social order in the new religious leaders and systems—Hinduism, Buddhism, Confucianism, the prophetic elements of Jewry, Zoroaster, Plato—which everywhere began to transcend the old limited vision of tribal animism. We cannot reduce any of the major elements in human experience to a simple projection of the others. They coalesce. They are also autonomous, and what is clear is that in the millennia of the great empires, religion was not only widened geographically to cover whole imperial systems. It was also elevated and refined. Possibly the advance of accurate measurement and the beginnings of technology reduced somewhat the scope of magic. But this is a minor point compared with a profound revaluation of man's relationship to the unknown.

We do not know why from one end of the world to the other the *external* religion of propitiation in which the gods are more or less bribed or appeased by gifts and offerings—including human sacrifice—gives way to a religion of the heart in which, as in the Confucian vision of the Way of Heaven, virtue is man's acceptable sacrifice, and what Montaigne was centuries later to call "an inner rule and decorum" is the only method of pleasing, propitiating, or indeed establishing any relationship with the Ground of Being. And this ultimate Fact is Itself recognized to be not capricious and malevolent but good and just. The change may merely be the unfolding of an original human insight present in tribal society but overlaid by ignorance and fear. It may be that once the attempt is made to universalize religion and transcend its tribal limits, the moral teachers confront not species of men but man himself and find in him, universally, the evidence of conscience, the aspiration to virtue, the justice which consists in claiming for oneself no more than one concedes to others. But whatever the cause, the change is a fact and the concept of an internal moral law begins to transcend the external magic and propitiation of tribal religion.

When we turn to function in the new age of empire, one thing at least does not greatly change. The chief source of wealth is still the land. To this one must now add mining to a much greater extent. On top of these basic activities there is raised, however, a completely new superstructure. It is more elaborate in technology. Water power increases output and demands wider administration. This in turn calls for new roads and new cities. Trade prospers as cities increase and distant provinces are opened up.

It is also infinitely more elaborate in hierarchy and class. New functions mean new skills, new officials, and new trades. At the top of society, the state-preserving professions of warrior, priest, and civil servant are the best rewarded and since land is the chief source of wealth, land revenues are often their income. Merchants making money by trade often buy into the land to increase their status. Tribal lands become the property of the chief turned territorial ruler. At the bottom, farmers and laborers do the heavy work. Slaves provide the menial labor in the towns. Above them, the families with property or status live off an economy to which they may or may not contribute a corresponding service in intellect or administration. This "feudal" economy continues to our own day.

In short, the result of the elaboration of technique and function in the great empires was to establish patterns of work and property of remarkable inequality and to replace the old undifferentiated tribal group with splendid, elaborate, unjust, and unstable systems which contributed as much misery as grandeur to the human experiment. The external instability of loyalties not wholly absorbed by conquest was matched at times by internal instabilities of peasant and class revolt. In spite of their wealth and magnificence, the empires proved remarkably perishable. The rise and fall of dynasties, conquests, wars, and rumors of war fill the millennia of their dominance. It is almost as though the combination of external and internal instability compelled them, like the Buddhists' "melancholy wheel" to a perpetually renewed cycle of rise and decay. The great leader, the effective dynast, the successful warrior recreates the state, extends its sway over the debatable lands between his system and the next, and the empire enters a phase of glory. But it overreaches its strength, the dynasty falters; its growth has aroused fear and mobilization among its neighbors; disintegration sets in until some new leader and some new power center arise. Any commentator looking at the civilized world some two thousand years ago would have seen little but this ebb and flow of empire—Egypt and the Hellenic empire ebbing, Rome rising, China at a zenith, North India recovering breath. He would have foreseen a continuance of these patterns into the future—possibly as far into the future as tribalism fell back into the past. But he would have been wrong. The first movements of a new phase were already under way.

Chapter Five

# Hellas and Jewry

IN ONE sense, the Greeks and the Jews were small peoples, not much beyond the tribal stage of organization, who, like hundreds of other small communities, were washing about in the slipstream of great empires. The Jews are absorbed for a time by Egypt, for a time by Babylon. Later they lose all identity under the Romans. The Greeks fought off the Persians, tried their own experiment under Alexander, and like the Jews ended up under Rome. Later they went through two more imperial experiences—under the Byzantine Empire and then the Turks. Like all small peoples living in the debatable lands between world systems, their own fortunes seemed to follow helplessly the movements of their mighty neighbors.

But they are unlike any other small peoples. If we ever feel discouraged about the apparent constraints on humanity, about its lack of elbowroom and freedom of action, we should think of the Jews and the Greeks, insignificant, powerless, and tiny in the age of the dinosaur empires, yet providing the growing points for the next stage in human destiny. In fact, to return to the analogy of evolution, if we could see man's historical development as a process akin to his biological evolution, we would see that certain events, communities, and even men are the points of mutation at which a decisive new direction may be introduced. The unpredictability, the unconstrained character of these changes lessens our sense of man bound to an iron wheel of fate. The past does not always condition the future. Art as well as science, inspiration as well as strict causality, choice as well as conditioning have built the human record. We should not despair.

The original contribution made by these two peoples of genius concerns the first of our two strands of cohesion—kinship and ideology. They did not make any changes in the economic field of function that had not been made elsewhere and by others. True, both peoples became very active traders and at one turning point in Greek history, the leaders consciously broke the dependence of Hellas upon traditional agriculture and launched it on a commercial career. But neither the way trade was conducted, nor the organization of farm work through slave labor, nor the techniques of agriculture differed much from those used in the neighboring empires.

The Greeks gave the world a new concept of the cement of the state, a new concept of what could hold the community together. This was the loyal acquiescence of free men making their own laws for themselves. No such possibility had been ever considered before. True, there are some intimations of it in tribal society where the tribal elders traditionally provide some restraint on the tribal chief and make up an element of consultation. In English political history, the Witenagemot, the old tribal council of the Anglo-Saxons, was one of the elements that went later into the making of the British Parliament. But this tribal pattern left little room for innovation since the elders had the primary task of preventing violations of tribal custom.

What the Greeks brought into society was the potentially dynamic principle that the citizen is free not only because he obeys laws but because he frames and changes them. Law as a means of orderly innovation and law as the safeguard of the citizen's freedom vis-à-vis government are inherent in the experiment of the Greek polis and both were genuine breakthroughs to a new concept of loyalty and cohesion in society. When the Greeks looked round at the dinosaur empires—including their nearest and most troublesome Persian neighbor—they called them barbarian because they did not live under law. They did not deny that their material culture was in many ways more elaborate than that of Greece. But their government was despotic and they were not free men.

The Greek contribution was no less startling in the

field of ideology or explanation. They inherited from
the old empires—from Egypt, from Babylon, from the
Chaldeans—a considerable amount of exact knowledge.
Astronomy, mathematics, and technology had all been
studied and used. The Greeks did not do much to carry
forward the technical application of this technology.
They were fascinated, instead, in the evidence it gave
of a vast orderly universe governed by law and acces-
sible to human reason. This grandiose vision of order—
which lies at the root of all modern science—would profoundly modify not only man's techniques but his whole
attitude to meaning and explanation. The sense of
malevolent gods and spirits behind volcanoes and earth-
quakes faded; the fears and confusions of animism re-
ceived a mortal blow. And the same vision, unforget-
tably portrayed in Greek poetry and drama, gave order
to man's moral universe. Every educated Greek child
learnt in Homer that the evils which befall mankind are
not arbitrary but rooted in the pride and rage of the
human heart. The arrogance of Achilles and the anger
of Agamemnon set in motion the whole drama of the
Iliad. The consequence of hubris is nemesis. The gods
may seem capricious or avenging. But we see Greek
thought struggling to see them as a mysterious expression of the causality of the universe in terms of man's
moral life. In this context, Greek thought is one of the
noblest and most rational expressions of the worldwide
turn toward a religion of internal integrity, not external
sacrifice.

It is also in this sphere of explanation or ideology

that we owe profoundly new insights to the Jews. One is a note of indignation and moral judgment found in no other culture. The Jews confront the enormous inequality of human society once it emerges from its tribal simplicity and proclaim God's profound concern for the poor. It is not simply that alms-giving is a duty—other cultures produce such obligations. It is that in some way the miserable and outcast are the Lord's chosen and deserve His especial blessing. Equally, the rich who accept their good fortune complacently are especially damned. If pride is the root of sin for the Greeks, hardheartedness and lack of compassion earn Jewry's chief anathema. This has injected a unique passion for social justice into the foundations of our later society.

The poor raised up, the afflicted restored to joy, an end to mourning—this apocalyptic picture of the righting of wrongs is not only an aspiration in Jewish thought. It is also an event. History is to move to such a consummation once "the former things have passed away." This is Jewry's second astonishing contribution to man's way of giving meaning to himself and to society. The Jews first planted in the world the explosive ideas of progress, evolution, and the ultimate "coming of the kingdom."

Resplendent as most of the world religions have been, magnificent as was their sweep and their scale, they nearly all end up with the somewhat despondent conclusion that history is repetitive and even meaningless. The life of society, like the life of man, completes itself in cycles of growth and decay and the chief wisdom of man lies in understanding these great recurrences and conforming to them. A note of resignation appears in the world philosophies—until we reach the Jews. Then the vision changes character entirely. The Jews look to the coming Parousia, to history's progress toward a messianic end of time. Meanwhile they work in history. The unfolding of history is the drama of God's purpose, and with an almost inconceivable audacity the Jews see man acting in this drama as co-partner with God Himself. This world becomes of infinite importance for it is the stage of the divine drama and the arena in which the final purpose of God will be revealed. Recurrence and passivity vanish. All is now dynamic change and active participation. It is as though the whole psychological bias of men's minds is being renewed.

Chapter Six

# The Nation-State

Bᴜᴛ ᴛʜᴇ profound signifi-
cance of Greece and Jewry is something we know by
hindsight. Their immediate fate was to be absorbed into
yet another of the dinosaur empires—the Roman Empire—and in the case of the Jews not to re-emerge as a
national community for nearly two thousand years.
Their presence inside the empire provided little observ-
able leaven of change. On the contrary, in its later stages,
the Roman system sloughed off all traces of republican-
ism and took on the features of divine kingship and
oriental despotism. Yet the leaven was there. Embedded
in the old imperial society was a system of cohesion and
explanation which has proved to be one of the greatest

forces shaping a new age in human history, an age which produced new kinds of community, new philosophies, and above all a wholly new range of economic functions.

This submerged system, which erupted to official influence just as the Roman Empire reached its term and then survived it, was, of course, Christianity. One could not at that time have foretold this innovating role. Its destiny might have been extinction, or if it survived, it could have become the religious philosophy and cultural mold of yet another imperial system. Something of this kind happened in Eastern Europe where Orthodox Christianity provided the religious core of two successive imperial experiments—the Byzantine and the Russian. But in Western Europe, the leaven began to work in quite new ways.

Why? There were apparently no a priori reasons of riches or climate. All the most prized forms of wealth were lacking—gold, jewels, spices. No one could then foresee what power was locked up in coal and iron. Compared with the old centers of civilization round the radiant Mediterranean, the new terrain of experiment seemed horribly bleak—dark forests, malarial swamps, rough seas, long winters, sunless climate, a barbarian people of whom contemporary civilized Muslims in Spain wrote that they were ugly, ungainly, dirty, with long hair and bad breath and—crowning horror—white skin. I think that at any time between the eighth and the fourteenth century, an observer from another planet would have been more likely to pick on China with its scale, its administrative order, rational temper, and elaborate civilization as the "lead sector" for human innovation rather than the chaotic, turbulent, and not yet very cultured peoples of Europe.

On the surface, medieval Europe might well have reminded Chinese historians of their own feudal troubles. There were the rival kingdoms dominated by a military and aristocratic caste, living off serf labor on the land and ruining themselves and each other in continuous warfare. The Chinese would no doubt have recommended to them the same pacification as was achieved in China—the establishment of a universal order bringing unity and an end to feudal strife. But this outcome was ruled out for Europe and the reasons explain why it was that, against all probability, the dark, forested, damp, and poverty-stricken Western tip of Eurasia turned into an irresistible growing point of new systems and new ideas.

No centralizing power proved strong enough to overcome the pluralism of feudal Europe. The Emperor fought for supremacy. So did the Pope. Neither won and no Byzantine fusion of authority could take place. At the same time, the legacy of the Greeks and the Jews returned to life in medieval Christianity. No doubt if a single centralizing power had been established, it could have overlaid the other energies just as Byzantium overlaid its empire. But in the loose, uncertain framework of Europe, Greek ideas of law and citizenship, and Jewish ideas of moral equality could be embodied in concrete ambitions and concrete groups. The merchant has made money all over the world and in every imperial order. In Europe, he was able to do more. He could achieve self-government. The cities were not splendid, segregated, administrative manifestations of the imperial cult. They were busy markets and centers of industry ruled by merchant corporations who had bargained privileges and charters out of Pope or Emperor in return for support and cash. They were centers, too, of learning in which civic universities began to flourish, beyond the direct control of either church or monarch.

Then came the decisive change. The Renaissance and the Reformation vastly reinforced both the secular knowledge and the political self-confidence of the rising middle class. They were now ready to produce the new forms of cohesion, explanation, and function which ended, presumably forever, the old unified empires and have dominated the world ever since.

The new political form of cohesion is the nation-state. One strand in this nationalism is not, of course, unique. Let us take Britain and France. Both are composed of original groups of tribes and were formed and reformed by waves of conquest, the last wave, Scandinavians from the North, carrying a last fling of conquest from Normandy to Britain in 1066. In the wake of these upheavals, the two communities framed particular languages and heightened each other's consciousness of separate statehood by their continuous feudal wars. One has only to read the early historical plays of Shakespeare to see how passionately antagonism to France shapes his sense of national identity: "Had death been French, death would have died today." But you could discover this cycle of consolidation and hostility on the rim of great empires in other parts of the world—for instance, the secular enmity of the Annamese and the Thais. But the nation-state did not begin in Southeast Asia.

What was unique in Western Europe was the thrusting up of new groups and classes to demand effective participation in the political life of the community. If they were to participate, they would have literally "to speak the same language." Literacy, education in greater depth, and the vernacular tongue ended the old split between ruling groups, often speaking an alien language, and the indifferent masses leaving politics to their betters. A community in depth began to form, conscious above all of its language as the bond of unity. And just because the whole of the community began to feel involved and to sense its difference from neighbors talking another language—the British and the French virtually created each other's nationhood by their constant hostilities—the new state began to relive at a much more powerful and elaborate level the old blood kinship of the tribe. The uneasy web of dynastic, hierarchical, and feudal relationships which had been the uncertain cement in the old dinosaur empires, gave ground before a new form of community—the agile, lively, strong, and sinewy societies of Western Europe, nation-states based on a single popular tongue and destined to bring *all* the people into a sense of near-tribal communion.

As power passed from the old centers of court and church and new groups rose to self-consciousness and power in the nation-states, new orders of explanation and meaning rose with them. What they have in common can best be described as the secularization of the old religious insights. In tribal religion all is "religious" because everything is still mysterious. Some of the great world religions were almost as closed to secular analysis and explanation. If the world is no more than a misery or an illusion, its actual workings hardly stimulate rational inquiry. But Christianity inherited the Greek sense of universal order and the Jewish belief in the value of time and creation. It attempted the distinction and balance between two valid orders—between God and Caesar, the sacred and the profane, between other-worldliness and the prayer "Thy Kingdom *come*."

The balance did not hold. Many of the master-ideas of the new dispensation had metaphysical roots—the equality of man, the belief in universal rational order, the sense of history as the unfolding of a progressive purpose. But now they took on a secular form. The rights of man replaced the equality of souls, scientific explanation the vision of divine order, biological and historical evolution the messianic hope.

Nowhere perhaps can one see more clearly the transformation of an originally religious idea into a profoundly wordly concept than in the thrust of the new economics. For the Puritan leaders of the Reformation—many of whom were drawn from the merchants and bankers and industrialists of the rising cities—the hard work and driving enterprise needed to build up a profitable undertaking were themselves God's work. If success and wealth followed, this would be a sign of God's blessing and approval. At the same time, they regarded all forms of spending as almost the equivalent of original sin. So they did not spend and thus held the delicate balance between God and Mammon. They also gave the world, almost by inadvertence, a perfect recipe for capital accumulation. It is even possible that without this attitude, Europe would never have acquired enough capital to launch the capitalist system.

As wealth accumulated and the system spread, the Puritan restraints began to wane. Hard-driving enterprise and money-making did not need to justify themselves in terms of industry and thrift. In fact, in the nineteenth century, in the first flush of the Darwinian theory of the survival of the fittest, ruthlessness itself became a virtue. The tougher and the more aggressive a man was in business, the quicker he reached the top by whatever means, the more he was proving his ability to survive and to play his essential part in fulfilling the evolutionary pattern.

At this point, we reach the third of the transformations achieved in Western Europe—the transformation of the economy. It is doubtful whether the modern economic system based upon savings and technology would have ever come into being without the political frame of a nation-state. Other factors were indisputably important—the passion for technology and gadgetry which has deep roots in Europe, the cult of natural sciences in the eighteenth century, the need, imposed on Europe by its apparently meager resources, to get out and trade overseas. But all these needs and activities had to find the right context, and this was the nation-state.

First of all, so long as politics were based on diverse, diffuse imperial systems with a whole array of minor authorities claiming undefined jurisdictions, it was very difficult to define the market. Again and again along the line of trade, the merchant would meet unpredictable taxes and embargoes and irrational interferences of every sort. Equally in most imperial systems, the monarchs had a certain tendency to raid their subjects' coffers—for war, for a new capital city, for a new mistress. To accumulate wealth under these conditions almost invited a robbing of the nest. A tremor of uncertainty ran through the old societies. Although merchants could grow rich, they tended to stow their money away in gold they could bury or jewels that could easily be carried across frontiers. In Latin America, today, the equivalent of all outside capital coming into the continent during the fifties was sent out again to bank accounts in New York and Switzerland. The attitudes persist. They do not build modern economies.

But in the nation-state, with an increasingly dominant merchant banking and middle class, private savings could be protected. The English civil war was, in a sense, an attempt to put back checks on the king's propensity to tax. Equally, it was possible to define the market and rid it of local cesses and taxes. For example, all through the seventeenth and eighteenth centuries, the road systems of Britain were beginning to improve. In the eighteenth century, national banking began to spread right through the country. Industry needed no longer to consist of workshops serving a village or a town or a river basin. It could begin to extend to a whole country. By defining the market, and by securing the market from undue intervention by the government, there was created an area wide enough and coherent enough for the industrial experiment to begin.

We should note, too, that it was internationally a competitive market. The British merchants, competing grimly with rivals across the Channel, acquired a much greater sense of their own identity and a much greater interest in the whole vast expansion of foreign trade which was one of the great engines of the European transformation.

This trade began as a series of attempts to impose and preserve nationalist, mercantilist monopolies. Throughout the seventeenth and eighteenth centuries, wherever you look on the map, you will find Portuguese fighting Dutch, Dutch fighting British, British fighting French, from one end of the world to the other. They fought each other to monopolize the slave trade; they maneuvered each other in and out of the Spice Islands; they chased each other round the Cape of Good Hope and up and down the Indian Ocean. Those old rivals in national self-assertion, the British and the French, were especially tenacious. The worldwide competition vastly increased both the risks and the enterprise of the system. It also vastly increased the profits. Both the money and the skills flowed back to Europe to provide the launching pad of the new technological and industrial system.

Of course the new system was a convergence of many factors—the growing interest in science and technology, the drive and resource of business entrepreneurs, the savings derived from foreign trade—but it is possible that the mix would never have produced the new economy without the nationalist drive and the national market. Equally it was in some degree nationalist rivalry that so quickly expanded the new system on a worldwide scale. All through Asia, European colonies were established, not primarily because colonies were the aim, but because each colonial power was maneuvering to keep other European rivals out. Similarly in Africa a century later it was nationalist competition that brought in the Powers. There were no large colonies in Africa before 1880—with the exception of the South, but there the Boers were settlers. After 1880, all the major European powers believed that if they did not annex territory, someone else would be there before them. Thus the Western colonial system, in spite of being the largest imperial system in history, resembles the old empires very little. It was less a purposive act of conquest than a by-product of national rivalry in Europe itself. By the same inadvertence it established a worldwide economic system.

## Chapter Seven

# Nationalism's Failure

THE nation-state has become the master-institution of our day. But such is the speeding up of the processes of historical evolution, that it is already difficult to believe that its dominance will last even the few millennia of the great empires. The very energies released by nationalism now undermine its validity and we seem to be moving, however uncertainly, into a new era of vast institutional change.

This is not to deny its profound and creative significance in human affairs. An astonishing release of energy, determination, and mental vigor was needed to transform the whole of the economic system of mankind from static farming to our modern dynamic technological system. They could not have been mobilized without this enormously potent propulsion of nationalism. Competition between national groups spurred the entrepreneur. Defining the national market gave him elbowroom. Even the worst consequence of combining nationalism and technology—the new destructiveness of war—has had its dynamic side. Modern war has brought about or accelerated most of our greatest technological innovations—internal combustion, flight, tank into tractor, electronics, atomic energy. Its total demands on the economy have also demonstrated the inconceivable productivity of our new techniques. When between 1940 and 1944 the United States doubled its existing industrial capacity, it showed that a couple of years were enough to build the equivalent of a century's growth. Only war could produce such accelerations, for only war provides—at this stage—a sufficiently overwhelming political purpose and consensus.

In politics, too, it may well be that without the new sense of a *national* community, we might not have achieved the successful breakthrough toward the popular vote, toward the admission of every citizen to equal political rights. Considering how deeply rooted many of the old feudal relationships have proved to be, possibly only a national community with its almost tribal sense of kinship could have evolved ideas of "the general welfare" and have brought about our contemporary widening of education and opportunity.

Yet for all its energy and creativeness, nationalism as an organizing principle fails in all three areas of human need—kinship, cohesion, and economic function. It gives us no answer to the problems of human solidarity and human community in areas where Western Europe's exceptional coincidence of language and frontier do not exist. In fact, in most of the world, particularly in the disputed lands left behind by old empires, the local communities are fragmented and divided. Southeast Asia, the Middle East, most of Africa are much more like the Balkans than Atlantic Europe. This fragmentation aggravates the problems of the imperial aftermath. When the Turkish empire began to crumble in the Balkans, the nation-states built on the basis of those mixed societies proved hopelessly unstable. Slav and Teuton and Magyar all lived huggermugger—and no nation-state could be built that did not include large disgruntled minorities. These were then exploited by outside contenders—Germany and Russia—and helped to precipitate two world wars.

Nationalism is thus not a wholly workable element of cohesion *inside* the state. Still less can it confront creatively our modern condition of more than a hundred states coexisting in inescapable physical proximity and economic interdependence. And this lack in turn points to its insufficiency as an order of explanation or meaning. Its essential nature is to leave other people out. This alone is not fatal. After all, that indispensable institution, the family, is also exclusive. But, save in a few societies, it hardly claims exclusive loyalty and authority. But nationalism has such pretensions. Moreover, it can back them with the ultimate choice of life or death. It can even divorce from all community of brotherhood and goodwill fellowmen who simply happen to live on the other side of a river.

The irrationality of which it is capable, because of such claims, has been demonstrated in our own day by the Nazis. They made the nation-state their god; it turned out to be a Moloch, because the extent of its claims contradicted the physical and economic and human realities within which the modern German community—like every other community—has to live. The claims could therefore only be put forward by literally deranged minds. However, once men lose all grip on reality, there seem to be no limits to the horrors of hatred and passion and rage they can dredge up from their psychological depths, horrors which normally we use all our social institutions to check. Unleashed nationalism on the contrary removes the checks. We have to remember that the obverse side of the comfort of tribal unity is the evil of tribal warfare. The stranger as enemy simply because he is the stranger condemns the world to the basic acceptance of disorder and to a continued toleration of all-out war. In tribal days, this ferocity decimated regions but not continents. In Hitler's day, it brought the world to the brink of destruction. In the day of the hydrogen bomb, it would push humanity over the edge.

Least of all, perhaps, can the nation-state still remain the master-institution of our new economic universe. Technologically the national market, which was big enough to be the forcing house of development at the end of the eighteenth century, has proved, for the last fifty years and more, too small to underpin full development. The British could use a small island base because they started first and had the world as an open, unimpeded area of operation. But of the powers who came after, only the United States had the continental scope needed for full success. Germany, cramped inside other people's tariff walls in Europe, twice plunged the world into war in order to secure more lebensraum. And the combined inability of all these separate, national economies to coordinate their policies in the wider world economy—on which all depended—led in 1929 to the Great Depression, a worldwide collapse of trade and confidence out of which mankind pulled itself only by the even more fatal expedient of war.

This suggests that, for all its energy, innovation, and vitality, nationalism is not a sufficient principle of cohesion, explanation, and economic function to cope with the consequences of its own success. It has destroyed most vestiges of earlier orders—the tribes are receding, the empires remain only where, as in China and Russia, they have gone far to transform themselves into nationstates. But it has not yet shown that it can be the active principle of a new social order wide enough in political institutions, human loyalties, and economic coordination to match a world made scientifically and technologically one. Once again, the human experiment faces revolutionary choices—but with the new and terrifying risk that this time, wrong choices may be final.

## Chapter Eight

# A Post-National
# Attempt: Capitalism

THE curious paradox is that, almost from the start, nationalism was felt, in an obscure way, to be an insufficient basis for the very forces—of democracy, of technology, of scientific curiosity and explanation—which the nation-state had helped to unleash. The two great earth-shaking revolutions of the eighteenth century set their sights high above the local community. The Founding Fathers and the French Jacobins share the same rhetoric. They speak for Man, for his inalienable rights, for his freedom and equality, for the universal validity of the claims he may justly and rationally make to life, liberty, and the pursuit of happiness. It is a time of universalism and also of an enormous optimism centered not on states or institutions or nations or governments but on the almost limitless potentialities of man himself. One hardly needed to be a poet to feel, with Wordsworth,

> Bliss was it in that dawn to be alive,
> But to be young was very heaven.

The mood of universal humanism and hope extends to all the instruments of community—kinship, function, meaning. Man freed from the fetters of a feudal, priest-ridden past will freely make the political decisions which serve his and his neighbor's interest. These, in any case, will not contradict each other, for a rational deity has "bid self love and social be the same." It follows that impediments to success and efficiency in the growing market economy do not lie with the divided minds and mixed motives of the entrepreneurs. Men, argues Adam Smith, are rarely so harmlessly employed as when they are making money. The obstacles to success lie in the determination of governments to restrict their citizens and to tie them down within narrow mercantilist limits. Free the entrepreneur and the new lively experimental forms of capitalism will surge ahead to create a world-wide environment of expansion, a "great commercial republic," in Adam Smith's phrase, a community transcending all local interests and leading, in its more hopeful supporters' estimate, to a new international climate of peace and cooperation. This dream—of enlightened self-interest rising above mercantilist repression and hostility and building a world of good neighbors—long sustained free traders like Cobden and Bright and tempted Tennyson to his vision of "the federation of the world and the Parliament of Man."

And beneath this faith in man's ability to achieve liberty in his politics and to build a free market economy lies a still deeper faith in his rationality and perfectability, in his reason and capacity for progress, once the old repressions are repealed. He was "born free and is everywhere in chains." Remove the inhibitions and he will be seen again in the calm, radiant light of his Hellenic morning. At the time of the Revolutions, the classical vision invaded not only men's art and architecture and dress and style, but their profoundest vision of human order.

Democracy, the free market mobilizing savings and technology, automatic progress—these were among the most potent forces of the nineteenth century and they virtually bypass the tough, institutional problem of how a worldwide system based on these forces will in fact work. The nation-state is taken for granted where it exists, and the new lava flow of democracy is poured into it. The old surviving empires are depth-charged with rising claims to popular sovereignty. Yet by a paradox, where Europe's nationalist interests clash—in Asia, in Africa—peoples are taken over and colonized largely to keep other nations out. One man's nationalism becomes another man's servitude. Only where earlier forms of government lay very lightly on a vast, empty land—in

America—did a political experiment emerge which was concerned with institutions *between* states in the new age.

First the confederation, then the federation were tried out in the United States to combine the security and opportunity of scale with the familiarity and appeal of the local community. Indeed, the young republic promised in every way to be a new phenomenon. It began without any tribal, imperial, or national past. Were it not for the dark stain of slavery and the dispossession of the Indians, one might almost talk of it as a state whose conception was immaculate. It looked forward to a new age from the day of its foundation. There was, by definition, nothing parochial or exclusive about its vision. Its truths were held to be "self-evident" to reasonable men everywhere, its citizens dedicated not to a blood tie or even a particular history—but to that most abstract and universal of symbols, a "proposition" about the fundamental nature and destiny of man. The United States began therefore as a new kind of state in which popular rights, self-determination, the open market, and the dream of progress offered a tremendous liberation from the past and a compelling pattern for the future.

This messianic strain has not been entirely lost under the realities and disappointments of actual history. The United States has continued to feel that a wider significance underlies its crises and struggles. The war to hold the Union together was also a war to convince the human race of the possibility of popular government. The war of 1917 was a war to make the world itself safe for democracy and after both world wars, the Americans took the lead in drafting the first sketch of a worldwide government—in the League of Nations and then the United Nations. In short, the first state to come into being fully and completely in the modern age is already very different in style and philosophy from the nation-states of Europe which brought the modern age into existence. From the start, its bonds of kinship have been rooted not in the local community but in the idea of man himself, its economic activities on the new abstract theories of supply and demand operating in a free, uncontrolled, and hence potentially universal market, and its sense of meaning in human equality and progress, in other words, in a secular version of Christianity's vision of man's metaphysical value and messianic hope.

That these new forces have proved totally and continuously revolutionary is not in doubt. The speeding up of the processes of change—from eons of tribal life to the millennia of the empires to the centuries of the nation-state—has begun in the modern age to make change itself the normal condition of human life. No state, market, or way of life—unless perhaps we exclude the Amazonian Indians—has avoided the flux of continuous adjustment and readjustment imposed on man by the reach both of his ambitions and his knowledge. But the revolutions have not had all the effects the original prophets of the revolution expected.

The universalist vision of free votes, free markets, and free men disturbed but did not entirely supplant a number of venerable and deeply rooted institutions. In

Europe popular sovereignty—the claim to govern one-self—neither weakened the nation-state nor led to some local version of "the federation of man." On the contrary, the fact that every citizen could feel a stake in the political decisions of his country vastly reinforced nationalism in the states of Western Europe and created new nation-states to the East of them. Old feudal units of government surviving in the ghostly frame of the "Holy Roman Empire"—that last pale reflection of ancient organization which Christian Europe had contrived to evade—broke away to form the German Reich or join in a united Italy. In the two empires in which a shot-silk texture of national minorities prevented any easy transformation into monolithic nationalism—the Austro-Hungarian and Ottoman empires—the new national forces hastened political decay and "Balkanization" and encouraged the Russians and the Germans to compete for the inheritance—a competition which led to two world wars.

Adam Smith was defeated in a similar fashion. As the nineteenth century advanced, it became quite clear that mercantilism was not dead. It had simply changed its board of directors. Under the old mercantilism, the state had manipulated the merchants to achieve its own monopolistic purposes. Under the new mercantilism, the businessmen used the state to achieve theirs. Only in Britain—which had a head start in competitive industrialism—did the vision of unfettered markets survive. In Europe, the new industrialists argued that they could not compete against Britain's greater economic strength and experience. They claimed protection for their own national markets and by a simple repression which Freud was later to make understandable, tariffs, subsidies, and quotas to protect local markets simply fell out of the consciousness of free enterprisers. They evolved a philosophy of governmental non-intervention save in the most critical of all categories—the fundamental definition of the size of the market. There they accepted, indeed, they insisted upon total governmental determination. The result was to build into modern capitalism almost as many roadblocks as the octroi, local taxation, and princely bribes had offered to the old feudal system.

In theory it is possible that an unfettered, worldwide market might have produced the peaceful, creative expansion of trade forecast by Adam Smith. But no law of nature rules that a hundred competing sovereignties will produce the same result—especially when the material interests of all the citizens become more and more engaged in the defense of the national market. So long as ninety per cent of the people were engaged in food-producing, largely for themselves, they had no particular stake in the economic activities of governments or of a tiny merchant class. But industry engages everybody. It gives back to the nation some of the communal involvement of the tribe. So war to protect the new system calls on everyone's loyalty and becomes in fact "total" in a wholly new sense. Thus nationalist economic rivalry reinforced by popular involvement became one thread—though only one—in the increasing aggressions of the early twentieth century and, between the two world wars, cutthroat economic competition carried on behind rival tariff walls helped to precipitate the temporary collapse of the capitalist system in 1929.

This survival and strengthening of nationalism occurred even in the state born out of due national season. America's response to the national rivalries and feudal survivals of Europe was, of course, to withdraw. In isolation, it conquered its continent. In isolation, it carried forward a version of its universalist dream by welcoming to its shores men and women from every nation under the sun and giving them the chance to become free citizens of a great republic. In isolation, it nursed its sense of a particular destiny—that of precedent and model in a world of freedom. And from the first, the organizers of the new community rooted its economic policy in a certain isolation by setting up a tariff structure tough enough to insulate the growing American economy from the competition of outsiders.

In part because of this isolation, the United States gives us a kind of clinically pure example of both the strength and the weakness of nationalism in the modern age. The strength lies in the degree to which a vast political experiment without any trace of tribal or national antecedents took on, over the decades, more and more of the characteristics of a *national* community. The sense of Americanism had to be developed. It was, in a sense, the fire under the melting pot. The creed remained universal but the flag, the oath, the school, the lengthening history, the separate myths, the all-American battles and struggles, the traumatic, unsharable experience of the Civil War—all these built up an Americanism which had all the pride and passion of earlier nationalisms and all the exclusions and rejections as well. After a hundred years of history, the community "dedicated to a proposition" was dedicated still more to the American way of life.

And since it has become in so many ways indistinguishable from a nation-state, it provides a unique yardstick for judging the effectiveness of the nation as the ultimate unit of loyalty and obedience. If the nation-state could be completely effective anywhere, it would be so in the United States. The moat which Shakespeare saw defending Britain "against the envy of less happier lands" was now two oceans between America and the world's troubles. The local lack of resources which sent the British all round the world in search of materials and opportunities for investment turned in America into a vast continent commanding one of the earth's largest expanses of rich temperate farming land and some of the greatest known concentrations of mineral resources. The alliances, the associations, the hang-over of aging institutions and traditions which caught Europe's separate states in a web of anachronism—all were lacking in America as an all but classless people turned their faces West to open up the opportunities of a continent. If one could live on this earth, unfettered by external commitments and pressures and therefore in an environment which is entirely under *local* control, America would be the place and a sovereign American community would provide all the bonds of kinship, function, and philosophy that men require if they are to live at peace and at ease with their fellow men.

Yet the world crowded in—and America crowded out. The giant economy that had grown up by the end of the nineteenth century began spilling its savings, its sales, and its purchases over the entire globe. By the twentieth it was on the way to becoming, behind its high tariffs, the world's largest creditor and the world's largest salesman as well, a condition which began to create havoc with the idea of self-balancing, self-financing, and self-managing world trade. If foreign countries were to repay interest and principal on American loans, they could do so only as they had repaid the British—by shipping out foodstuffs, raw materials, and manufactures. But the Americans had become, unlike the British, massive exporters of everything. They not only lent more than they borrowed. They sold more, too. Between the wars, the gold began to pile up in America from repayment of debts unpayable in goods.

The earlier supposedly automatic working of the gold standard faltered. Uncertain liquidity in world trade, coupled with higher tariffs in Europe and shrinking demand for primary products everywhere, caught the world economy in a downward spiral of shrinking demand. Not all the basic strength and resources of America could hold it aloof from the 1929 Depression in which world trade fell to a third of its old volume and unemployment leapt up to twenty and thirty per cent of the labor force.

And since the world economy was supposed to run automatically *without* government intervention, no agreed policies for recovery could be worked out. Demand heavily revived in one field only—the production of arms. In one decade after the Depression, Europe was again at war and basically for the reasons of 1914—the inability of rival, distrustful nation-states to accept the risk that one or other of their number should gain *more* national power in the post-imperial twilight zone of Central and Eastern Europe.

And again, as in the earlier war, the United States could not hold aloof. If Germany, either in 1914 or 1939, had been able to restore the old system of empire and draw together the richest, most skilled, most educated, most forceful communities of the world in a single complex of power under German imperial organization, no other community would have been secure. If Russia and Germany struggled over the uncertain inheritance of power in the Balkans, America and Germany could be said to be struggling over the dubious inheritance of power in the whole of Europe.

True, the Americans, like the British in the Napoleonic wars, intervened not to impose their own control but to prevent a take-over bid by another nation. But the facts of power dictated their intervention since the prizes and the risks were much too formidable to be left to go by default. The challenge to American self-interest at this stage could no longer be contained inside the isolationist formula. In 1917 and 1941, the United States entered the world's wars just as in 1929 it was drawn into the world's depression. Not even the most successfully self-sufficient nation in human history could contract out of the global society—of technology, of worldwide trade, of total communication and interdependence—the nation-state had helped to build.

Meanwhile, the ideology of free markets and free enterprise had run into difficulties and contradictions *inside* the national community. Some seemed inherent in the new processes of production. The early economists saw clearly that the big engine thrusting the new system forward was enterprise powered by profits. But the market itself cannot automatically guarantee their growth and continuance. To produce something uses up skills and resources and to sell it satisfies demand. A point comes when materials and labor become more scarce and expensive and the products more costly to put on the market. Meanwhile people who have already satisfied their needs are no longer so anxious to buy. Costs rise, prices fall, and down go the profits. Push the dilemma far enough and the whole inducement to produce vanishes.

Yet the brutal answer of keeping labor costs low by exploiting a bewildered, first-generation urban proletariat could not be a final answer. It might permit the organizers of the new system to secure the massive savings they needed to get the first machines and factories and roads and harbors all built. But a poor proletariat cannot buy enough goods to create a dynamic market. Even if costs are held down, purchasing power does not go up—so profits fall by another route.

These were some of the dilemmas which haunted the classical economists. Whichever way round they twisted the system, a contradiction, cutting profits and hence dynamism, seemed to come up. This earned them the title of "dismal" scientists. But it would have required peculiar clairvoyance for them to have remained as buoyant and cheerful as Adam Smith. They could not foresee the stupendous productivity of the new energy, the new machines and discoveries. They could not know how quickly the whole world would be drawn into the web of supply—cheap wheat from the New World drawn in to redress the costly corn of the Old. They could not guess what a vast range of new products could be invented to tempt the most jaded consumer. They could not know because they did not believe that massive governmental interventions would increase production by war efforts and redistribute income by taxation. The system had, in short, far more flexibility than the original theories allowed for.

Yet their analysis, within its own terms, could not be called irrelevant. As believers in free enterprise, they had to discount government. Their mercantilist experience left them convinced—as many men remain to this day—that its interventions would distort the market and do more damage than good to the economic system. And if one excludes all public economic decision-making, one has left only the private decision-makers and their judgments about profitability to guide the economy.

From the start, these private decisions led to considerable instability in the economy—the business cycle did represent an upward movement of growth while demand was unsatisfied and resources and skills were still not stretched to the limit, and then a downward movement as costs rose on the supply side just as demand began to fall on the other. On the whole, this rhythm of expansion leading to inflation and of contraction leading to a deflated economy left the tide of growth farther up the world's beaches after each temporary retreat. Overall wealth grew—although at an uneven pace. But between the wars, the Great Depression suggested that the central mechanism had become, in some way, stuck. Savings piled up in bank accounts, farmers burnt coffee and ploughed corn under, men and women tramped the streets in search of work—but capitals, resources, and labor could not be brought together because the profit mechanism as the sole energizer of the economy had slipped out of gear.

The reason was, of course, that in those traumatic days, so many different sources of demand—postwar reconstruction, primary incomes, the American boom of the twenties, the openings for trade in tariff-ridden Europe—had all failed at once. Businessmen, facing a worldwide absence of markets, had no inducement to invest since they saw little prospect of selling. The profit motive could not reactivate an economy from which the stimulus to expand production had been removed. The stimulus finally came from the most tragic source—from production for war.

It is from this time that we can date the gradual turning away of capitalist economics from the old dream of purely automatic, market solutions. In practice, if not wholly in theory, the market economies have moved not, certainly, to abolish the concept of profits—which remain the chief yardstick of efficient productive performance of satisfying the consumer's real needs—but to set them in a wider context of maintaining steady demand and hence steady employment in the whole economy. It is the responsibility of government and business together to see that demand rises fast enough to employ all the economy's resources and to stimulate the expansion of new research, capacity, and skill. But the advance must not be so fast as to get ahead of existing capacity and force up prices toward inflation.

Such a balancing act is very far from easy. Sudden changes in the harvest, new fundamental inventions, the scarcities due to political crises, immobility in parts of the economy, the bidding up of wages for temporarily scarce skills—all these keep the economy in a constant tremor of fluctuation and the countervailing action has to be delicate, sophisticated, and continuous. The policy is also new and not yet fully grasped. Moreover, some large elements used to sustain demand in the Western world look a little dubious when one remembers that they include eighty billion dollars a year spent on arms. In a sane world, one could conceive of less lethal instruments of "demand management." Even so, it can be said with increasing certainty that after two centuries of operation, free enterprise in the free market has both proved its extreme efficiency as a producer of goods and also its need to be balanced, supplemented, and supported by a measure of external public direction. The dream of Adam Smith has not proved wholly mistaken. But men know now that in economics as in every other human sphere, the perfectly self-functioning and self-regulating activity belongs to the world of archangels, not of men.

These dilemmas have been concerned with the ability of the free market system to produce material goods in plenty. Another set raise the issue of its ability to distribute them once they are produced. The great revolutionary ideologies of America and France had nothing very specific to say on this critical question of distribution. Presumably the market would take care of it, but there was no hint of how the process would work out, or even of how it ought to work out—unless the Jeffersonian and French commitment to "equality" covered more than political status and equality before the law. In fact, both revolutions ignored and could not help ignoring the extraordinary divide in history and in institutions upon which they stood. Behind them lay the accumulated traditions and patterns of the static hierarchical feudal-imperial societies which the nation-state had been hammering to pieces. Before them lay the new shapes of a mobile, dynamic, unhierarchical market economy which they could hardly yet even discern. Both the outgoing inheritance and the incoming energies imposed on the ideology of free markets and free enterprise a number of tough dilemmas which, it can be argued, it has not completely resolved, even today. And most of them concern distribution.

All over the world, before the coming of science and technology, there was only one principal source of wealth and means of producing more wealth—the land. From the break-up of tribal society, land had been largely used to provide income for the leaders of society—princes, warriors-turned-dukes, churchmen. In such land-based societies, even men who made money in trade tried to buy land to achieve the highest respectability. At the beginning of the age of nationalism, Tudor adventurers turned monastic lands into great fiefs. Four hundred years later, local merchants and entrepreneurs in the Westernized cities of China were still ploughing their profits back into "ancestral" estates in their native villages.

But in Europe, the security of the cities and the increasing liveliness of trade built up more diverse and dynamic means of production. A man with entrepreneurial intelligence, organizing this group of workers in this town quarter to spin yarn for weavers in another and selling the cloth all across Europe began to own, under the general head of capital, the buildings, the materials, the completed stock, and the working capital needed to carry it from its first working-up to the final sale. As the length of time used both in producing and exchanging goods increased, the amount of capital needed to "buy" this time increased too and banking institutions spread rapidly to provide, at a price, the necessary finance.

Compared with the solid definitions and obligations of the old landed property, this new partly rooted, partly mobile property of "capital" seemed difficult to bring into a coherent social theory. Aquinas had said that man had the right to own property because he could take better care of it—but that he held it on trust. A good landlord recognized obligations to tenants, to workers, and to the fertility of the land; a bad landlord rack-rented his people and spent the proceeds in riotous living. But this theory presupposed a direct and recognizable link between owner and dependents. John Locke tried to provide the justification of the new, strangely impersonal property that lay in part along the whole process of production and in part was piling up in banks and countinghouses. Resources and labor were, he pointed out, inert and valueless until the entrepreneur set them to work. By adding this dynamic element of enterprise, men turned useless stuff or unused energy into a productive force able to satisfy demand in an active market. In this capacity lay the ultimate right to own the new forms of property—since they simply did not exist until the factor of enterprise had been added.

Or one could approach the problem from the side of saving. As the processes of production and then of marketing began to lengthen, they demanded more and more credit to finance the entrepreneur right through from the purchase of his materials to his final sales. He had therefore to find people who were prepared to postpone their own consumption and hand him over, for immediate use, the money which represented their own claims on the economy's resources. Clearly this money was their personal property, and invested in an enterprise, its character presumably did not change, whether they lent it for a limited time at a fixed price or threw their lot in for good and ill with the new enterprise and became part "owners" in return for a division of the ultimate profits.

At first, if the enterprise failed, they had to stake their whole fortune to pay off creditors. But limited shares—or liability—appeared in Britain in 1863. Then they lost no more than the original investment. A man could have snippets of ownership in a score of companies. The system became still more impersonal when these small stakes themselves proved to be highly salable and interchangeable and men began to purchase them simply to profit by the fluctuations in their market price. Ownership which amounts to no more than a tiny share of a dynamic enterprise changing hands on the stock exchange is difficult to fit into any traditional concept of ownership as a trust or a responsibility. Nor is the Lockean argument entirely applicable, since a man could hardly be said to have added some essential quality of enterprise to inert matter if he had for a time speculatively held some stock in the hopes of a rise. Indeed, if the money he used to purchase the stock had come from inherited wealth, it could be argued that his own contribution was zero. Where then could the social justification for the rewards of ownership be discovered?

This is not to say that the whole new system of mobilizing capital was not brilliantly successful. After all, the central technique of the new economy lay, as Adam Smith had suggested, in its ability to break down the processes of production into their component parts, to specialize workers and machines on each stage, to apply to them a vast new range of energy and mechanical power, and at the end of the process to secure far more goods out of given applications of time, labor, power, and materials. But every aspect of this process demanded savings—or capital—to cover the lengthening time of the productive process and to finance the subtraction from daily consumption of the materials employed—in the coal mines, in the coal-fired steam engines, in the machines worked by steam, in the railways and trains which distributed the final goods. If people were not prepared to "not consume" on a very considerable scale, consumption would simply nibble away the resources which, saved, could go into the productive process and provide more consumption later.

In the first stages of modernization, in particular, before roads and railways are constructed, power plants installed, ports and cities built, and mass education of all kinds launched, the scale of "non-consumption" needed becomes for a time almost catastrophic, especially in poor countries where the margins available for saving can be unimaginably meager—a dilemma which the whole developing "South" of our planet is confronting now. So the discovery, by trial and error, of the market economy's capacity to mobilize vast amounts of saving must be rated an indispensable aspect of its successful working.

So was the unplanned but crucial fact that the first large increases in wealth made possible by the new technology tended to flow back to those whom society recognized as the property owners, the entrepreneurs, and the savers—banks, wealthy families, international merchants—who could afford to reinvest since they were already wealthy enough to satisfy their own needs. Thus the new system's ability to mobilize savings and channel them to the people who would use them and reinvest them was one more vindication of the early ideologues' hope that the laws of supply and demand operating in the free market—in this case the market for savings—would of themselves propel mankind if not into a new heaven and earth at least into a new economy.

Yet by identifying ownership—or property—in the new system solely with savings and entrepreneurial risk and skill, the new society of capital and technology unwittingly created for itself a quite unforeseen range of social and political problems. That the innovators and organizers of a new, still unknown system should be highly rewarded was rational enough. Great risks deserve great returns and in an uncharted economy, everything is risky. That the "savers" should share in the uncertain gains also made sense since they had to be persuaded to face the possibility of losing their stake. Nevertheless, dukes and bankers for whom saving was hardly a sacrifice also made up part of this group and one could hardly rate them as hardship cases. From the start, the free market operated on the biblical theorem: "to him who hath shall be given"—in itself an uneasy base for social peace. What created an even greater malaise was the sheer scale of the new dynamic wealth. The profits earned by successful enterprise, which in turn increased the market value of its share capital, poured wealth on a wholly new scale into the pockets of the organizers and savers. Profits virgin of all income tax, capital gains of monumental proportions poured out of the technological cornucopia and were funneled straight to the new entrepreneurial groups and to the old aristocrats who had had the wit to invest.

An Earl of Durham sitting on square miles of farm land underpinned with square miles of coal could, as he said, "jog along" on £40,000 a year. Others were less modest. The age of the tycoon dawned, men with personal fortunes on the scale of the national incomes of whole countries. True, they could be called the Himalayan peaks in the still small but rising range of middle-class fortunes. Yet one did not need to be very radical to feel industrial society was producing a rather peculiar profile of rewards and prizes. If one returned to the Lockean definition of property—that it "belongs" to those who add to inert matter the possibility of being used—what should labor earn? Should its rewards be wholly unrelated to ownership in spite of its indispensable contribution? Should a man who has added his work and skill enjoy no part of the capital gains that could not have been earned without him? The new processes of industry were essentially cooperative or collective. It seemed somewhat arbitrary to divorce one part of the team—the workers—entirely from the most dynamic section of the rewards.

If one turned further back—to Aquinas—the position became even more confused. What sense of trust or responsibility did a 7/500 part of an enterprise confer on the owner of this tiny segment? He felt none. Usually he demanded no more than that it should funnel to him his share of profits and capital gains. The notion of property as a trust vanished before such anonymity and such lack of anything save a cash interest.

Meanwhile the workers in the first decades of industrialism, uprooted from their traditional, dependent, but well understood life as country people, streamed into dismal cities to confront a system in which they were simply one factor of production in a competitive market. Their work could earn them the wages needed to stay alive and reproduce enough workers to keep the market supplied. Over and above that minimum, cutthroat competition to keep down costs would slice off any extras. Moves to mitigate hours of work or raise rewards could cut profits and hence switch off the energy of the whole system. Early economists might worry about some of the implications of this free market for labor. They might question whether wages would ever grow enough to create the mass demand needed to balance the growing productiveness of the machines. But within the framework of free markets and free enterprise, organized on the basis of concepts of property inherited from the past, there was no way out. An air of bafflement pervades a lot of the writing in mid-Victorian times. Honest observers could not miss the growing and appalling gap between the bounding wealth of the few and the depressed misery of the many. But this was how the market worked. Tamper with it and the whole system might break down.

Later on, as the new system spread to include sup-

pliers from all round the world, a comparable dispro-
portion began to develop between the wealthy white
North Atlantic market economies and the developing
continents to the South. And it sprang from some of the
same causes. Since Europeans and Americans took to
Asia, Africa, and Latin America the entrepreneurial skills
and the original capital for investment, they also pre-
empted the profits and the capital gains. All through the
Southern lands, modernized enclaves grew up round
mines and plantations and round the ports that were
used to ship minerals and coffee and copra and rubber
back to the developed "North." Local people provided
the labor and where there were too few, workers were
shipped in—Indians to British Guiana or Fiji, Chinese to
Malaya, Negroes everywhere—to spread round the world
a chain of troubled, racially plural societies.

Not much of the new wealth remained in local hands.
Profits, higher salaries, capital gains went back to the
outside investors and local expenditure was mopped up
by the sale of Western goods through expatriate concerns. In many colonies, business interests did not even
pay local taxation until after the Second World War. In
extreme cases, one could argue that the local inheritance
was no more than the hole in the ground where minerals
had once been taken out. In short, the free market, operating abroad within the same definitions of property,
produced both the same dynamism and some of the same
disproportions on a global scale

As the nineteenth century advanced, it became clear
that there *were* answers to the supposedly fundamental

"contradiction" of the free market—its inability, given its property structure, to spread to the mass of the people enough wealth and hence demand to mop up the mammoth growth of goods on the side of supply. The answer finally emerged neither from any large scale reordering of the market nor from any sharply revised structure of property. It came, in contradiction to the universalist and automatic ideology of the first economists, very largely from governmental intervention.

There were, it is true, other forces at work. Labor in a free society could combine to force up wages—and once workers displayed this power, it was quickly discovered that the system's fabulous productivity could absorb higher profits and higher wages too. It is also true that, as industrialism developed, the master-institution of the new system—the corporation—revised its managerial outlook to include a stable, well-paid, and contented labor force among its main sources of productivity. But from the first modest introduction of taxation to provide such basic services as popular education or housing on to the postwar governmental commitment to the maintenance of full employment, the government has intervened increasingly to redistribute wealth, to increase consuming power, and to make the maintenance of high demand in the economy a fundamental aim of policy.

In so doing, it has, of course, reinforced the power and authority of the nation-state and contradicted the vision of a universal economic order operating on more or less automatic and self-regulating lines. At the end of two centuries of the new technological economy and of its

spread to embrace the globe, we find a large enhance-
ment of local state power, a reinforcement of national
particularism. The external "mercantilism" of tariffs and
quotas has been reinforced by the internal consolidation
of planning, welfare, and popular economic involvement.
The ideologues of free enterprise have not been proved
wrong in their estimate of its dynamism, its productivity,
its radical ability to remake the face of the earth. But
they were dead wrong about its automatic and self-
regulating character. In its first outward sweep round
the world it has reinforced, not superseded, the authority
of the nation-state.

We are left at this point with the last of the visions of
the Enlightenment—faith in the automatic progress and
reconciliation that would flow once man was freed from
the fetters of the past—fetters of feudal government,
fetters of mercantilist economics, fetters of religious su-
perstitition. In many ways, the vision has been inconceivably reinforced. At no time in human history has
material progress been so stupendous. Magic has given
way forever before the magnificent structure of a science
which unfolds with each discovery the Greek vision of
an orderly and hence understandable and even controllable universe. The giant strides in physical health, the
vast advances in food production, the invention of energy which can be virtually self-perpetuating, the deli-
cacy of instruments which can photograph the dark side
of the moon and soon land men on other planets—all
these advances go so wildly beyond the furthest imag-
inings of the first men of science that no one in his senses

can deny the solid incontrovertible facts of almost inconceivable technical and scientific progress.

Yet this is a time of misgiving. It is simply a truism to say that the anxiety centers not on human power and inventiveness but upon man himself. Part of the anguish can be called theoretical. The great philosophical systems which have arisen since the euphoria of the Enlightenment all strike, when interpreted brutally and simply to public opinion, a pessimistic note about the nature and destiny of man. According to the popularizers, Marx makes man a reflection of property relations, Darwin of the survival of the fittest, Freud of an unknown libido. Each has in common a loss of control, a loss of self-determination, a loss, to revert to jargon, of the identity that comes from believing in free will. It is possible, in face of this belittlement, for man to say: "At least I have the illusion of choice. Even if my decisions are absurd, I become human by engaging and committing myself." But this is no longer the dawn in which it is good to be alive. It is the night in which nothing is left but the courage of despair.

And this philosophical loss of faith has been enormously reinforced by plain, brute experience. Horrors are hardly new in human history. When Ghenghis Khan left a pyramid of half a million skulls in Baghdad, he reached, proportionately, the Nazis' average. The new chill horror of concentration camps and genocide and purposive torture springs from the earlier belief that the "former things had passed away." Brutality, reinforced by scientific precision, is trebly horrifying after the decades of faith in progress. Today, the dream of the Enlightenment fades not only because the philosophical foundations have been knocked from beneath man's very ability to choose dignity, equality, or fraternity. It fades because man has in fact chosen the opposite—total abasement, total discrimination, total hate. Of all the legacies of the earlier revolutions it is perhaps their buoyant, unquenchable faith in man that has most diminished in the modern age.

## Chapter Nine

# A Post-National
# Attempt: Communism

THUS some sense of defeat
hangs over mankind's first attempt to construct a trinity
of kinship, function, and meaning appropriate to a post-
national, worldwide society. It is certainly not dissipated
by studying the counter-version of virtually the same
faith. The American and French Revolutions did not end
the traumatic upheavals of modern history. Revolution
in 1848, the Commune of 1871, Russian revolutions in
1905 and 1917, the victory of Communism in China in
1949—the crises continue, lineal descendants in one sense
of the earliest liberal revolution, yet rejecting and debat-

ing and fighting it with all the passion of heresiarchs offering the true, new, version of the old faith. For the gospel according to Marx is, to an uncanny degree, the mirror-image of the gospel according to Adam Smith or the Founding Fathers. They believed in limited government. He carried it to the pitch of the state "withering away." They believed in the automatic economy. He too believed it would run itself—once the inhibitions of profit and property were removed. They believed in irresistible progress toward a society in which men in full equality would enjoy life, liberty, and the pursuit of happiness. He believed in history leading to the millennium of the classless society. They are all children of the same Enlightenment and the chief difference between them is that, in the true spirit of the dialectic, Marx's vision is the critique, the counter-vision, the antithesis to the thesis firmly set by the earlier "bourgeois" revolutions. His ideology is inconceivable without its profound rejection of theirs. Yet in a strange way, it is the same ideology, the same profound commitment to a government and an economy so free that they run themselves and a certainty of progress so absolute that history itself will bring it about. They are both efforts to reach out to new forms of association, economic activity, and belief on a world-wide scale, on the basis of humanity itself. They both belong, in intention, to the post-national age. And they both fail before the tough inheritance and the tougher institutional necessities of actually working in a world of states.

The failure of the Marxist dream comes later in time

simply because it did not capture a working base until 1917. Up to the Soviet revolution, Communism's chief force lay in devastating criticism of the crude realities and disappointments of the liberal age. The fact that, as a product of the Enlightenment, it professed all the same ideals—equality, justice, progress, the use of science, the power of reason, the primacy of man—created the context of a real debate. For instance, the Marxists did not say: "You are on the wrong tack. Your vision of society is false. Only blood, soil, obedience, and hierarchy add up to a tolerable condition for man." On the contrary, they accepted all the liberal ideals and then turned a devastating broadside of criticism on bourgeois society's failure to realize them.

The attack, naturally, concentrated on those parts of the new system which most flagrantly violated the hope of justice, equality, and progress. Marx formulated his vision during the first period of "primitive accumulation" in Britain and Europe when, on the evidence of what statistics we have, little if any of the increasing wealth created by the new combination of savings, enterprise, and technology flowed back to the growing urban proletariat. Standards of living remained as low in 1840 as in 1800. As we have seen, under the concepts of ownership prevailing at that time, none of the wealth could have been channeled to the broader masses and this fact, awkward as it might be for the lovers of justice and equality, probably alone made possible the original breakthrough to massive saving. The workers would have consumed it; the entrepreneurs and bankers reinvested

( 89 )

it. The mechanism had not been consciously evolved but, in fact, in the middle of hideous misery and unbelievable deprivation, it began to work.

And this was the point at which Marx struck home. He allowed the entrepreneurs every credit for ingenuity and drive. He saw them as the midwives of a new age of triumphant technology and material liberation. He is almost as cheerful as Adam Smith about the vision of a world recreated and reconciled by its new economic possibilities. But the midwives are also strangling the child at birth. To breathe, to grow, it would need a market large enough to absorb its fantastic potential for producing goods. Marx was one of the earliest observers to guess the astonishing productivity of the new system. But channeling all the surplus, over and above the costs of production—the true profits—solely to the owners of private property meant, for Marx, that the necessary expansion of the market could not take place. On the contrary, the disequilibrium the system set up would lead, ineluctably, to the poor growing poorer and becoming less and less able to consume the economy's product. It would therefore founder in a series of crises of supposed overproduction, which would in fact be due to the inability of the masses to consume enough.

Nor could Marx accept Locke's justification of the rights of ownership. Quite apart from the feudal hangover of large-scale private ownership in the land—which Locke's theory in any case did not touch—Marx denied the preemptive rights of capital ownership. It was the addition of *work* to inert matter that made it useful and valuable. It was workers mining materials, workers building machines, and workers using the machinery who, all together, provided the essentially collective basis of the new wealth. To exclude from the dynamic rewards of the new system precisely the laborers who had made the rewards possible implied more than a technical failure, or an inability to achieve a proper expansion of demand. It was an act of appalling injustice, of conscienceless exploitation, of intolerable oppression, a crime "calling to Heaven for vengeance" since it deprived the worker of his hire and ground down the faces of the poor.

Inevitably, one uses the biblical idiom, for it is from the other, non-Hellenic strain in the Christian tradition that Marx, one of the greatest of the Jewish prophets, derives his power. His labor theory of value did not bear the interpretation he placed on it even at the time of its formulation and it has long since ceased to be of much interest save to keen amateurs of Marxist lore. Nor could his theory of the progressive impoverishment of the workers survive once governments began, after the 1850's, modestly at first but later more decisively, to intervene in the economy and secure a larger share of wealth for the masses. But the technical, or as he would have said, scientific aspects of his theory could wither without affecting the profound force of his moral invective. His attack on the vast and growing gap between rich and poor in the supposed dawn of equality and progress went back to roots which Christians could not ignore—the unique Jewish tradition of justice for the oppressed, of God's special concern for the poor and power-less, and of His special judgment on the indifferent rich.

Marx himself did not believe that the capitalist system could be modified. The men who privately owned the means of production and engrossed for themselves the vast dynamic gains of the new technology were the same men, in his view, who controlled the government, ma-nipulated the national market for their own purposes, and used the state itself as an instrument of private greed. Nor did Marx live long enough to devise any mod-ification of his theory when the extension of the franchise to most adult men began to increase vote-hungry poli-ticians' interest in making the workers not poorer but very much better off.

It was left to Lenin to rescue the theory of "pro-gressive impoverishment" by transposing it from the Atlantic heartland to the colonial and semi-colonial "Southern" continents. There, he said, the total exploi-tation of local workers and local resources was creating a surplus which, shipped back to Europe and America, gave even the workers a share in the exploitative gains of imperialism. But, he argued, the respite would be temporary. The cutthroat competition between pro-ducers to control a limited market which Marx had pos-tulated for the internal Atlantic economy would now be projected to the world at large and the capitalist states would compete with each other to monopolize inade-quate colonial markets and thus plunge mankind into a succession of imperialist wars. From this continuous ca-tastrophe deliverance would be achieved only by abandoning monopoly-capitalism and establishing the world-wide brotherhood of Communist man.

And in the event the first toehold of Communism as a counter-society, not simply a counter-theory, did occur in a society which had some things in common with the semi-colonial lands—foreign ownership of most of the modernized sectors, a small local proletariat, static agriculture, limited technical and scientific education, an alienated intelligentsia. All these factors in Russia conspired to create a state too unstable to withstand the hammer blows of war—just as they were to produce the same effect, some thirty years later, in China.

In 1917, the Marxists acquired a base and could begin, in Lenin's rhetoric, "to build socialism." Once again, a vast community had been established on the basis not of a tribe, a nation, or a history but on a belief or "proposition." Once again a state had been set up with a worldwide sense of its implications and its message. Once again, the attempt would be made to tailor a whole society to the new needs and aspirations of a universal faith. And, once again, the experiment failed and for many of the same reasons, above all the hopelessly utopian quality of its basic faith.

When it came to running the battered, war-torn Russian economy with its rural bias and its primitive industrialism, there was nothing in Marxism to tell the leaders how it should be done. Marx had assumed the existence of a complete capitalist structure which would begin to work smoothly as soon as the basic contradiction of distributing the profits only to private owners had been eliminated and the slogan "production for use, not profit" had taken its place.

Lenin had, it seems, a rather contemptuous idea of the entrepreneurial talents needed to run industry. It could be done, he said, "by pastry cooks." But it could not. When the brief years of War Communism in which workers tried to run factories ended in chaos, Lenin reintroduced private commerce and some private land-ownership in his New Economic Policy. It was left to Stalin to discover what socialism meant. He identified public ownership with state ownership and gave the government the task, on lines that recalled a Western war-economy, of building up industrialism by forced saving and public fiat. The mass of the people would save as fiercely as ever they did under capitalism, and the surplus would be siphoned off, from countryside and factory, into the creation of the infrastructure and industrial base of "socialism in one country."

The system worked. Enough of it was in place to survive Hitler's murderous attack. The country moved from the wooden plough to Sputnik in forty years. But in the course of working, it completely destroyed the Marxist vision of the vanishing state, the self-functioning economy, and the inevitable harmony of a new international system.

Take first the economy. By placing the entire system under governmental control and placing the entire investible surplus under the orders of the central bureaucracy, the Communists produced a state not in the process of withering away but of acquiring a greater concentration of power than any exercised by previous rulers in history. Where decisions were as large and "lumpy" as the system itself—coal mining, power, steel, heavy industry—the new bureaucracy managed well enough. Marx's passion for science was carried over into the state's dedication to research. The liberal philosophy triumphed in a massive extension of education—even if it was singularly absent from what was actually taught. But the state-run economy threatened from the start to be about as agile and flexible as a hippopotamus. War economics, siege economics—these it could cope with by brute strength. But after forty years of toil, the Russians began to expect more than a siege. They had gone through their phase of "primitive accumulation" and had its horrors repeated by the need to accumulate all over again to undo the inconceivable damage of invasion. Now, like the masses in the West a hundred years earlier, they wanted fairer shares.

At this point, the Communist version of the modern technological society began to meet its own contradictions. The trouble did not lie in the absorption of the surplus by the private property owners. There was nothing to stop any surplus from flowing anywhere the government might dictate. The trouble lay first in producing a genuine surplus, in other words, in inducing efficiency in output. It also lay in redirecting the flow of resources into that stream of multiple, changeable, insubstantial, fashion-dictated goods which consumers, given their own wishes, really want. For both purposes—efficient production and consumer choice—a centrally-planning bureaucracy on a continental scale seems about as unhandy and unresponsive an instrument as man can devise. And it is from this over-centralized system that the Russians are now trying to escape.

What we witness today is essentially the application to the Soviet planned economy of some facets of the market economy—profit as a yardstick of efficiency, decentralized management as a means of lively response to market pressures. Whether the new ability of Soviet managers to use the profits they earn for local bonuses and rewards will end in a sort of corporate private ownership, we do not know—just as we do not know whether profit sharing, stock ownership by workers, pension funds, and the vast growth of insurance may not end by creating a species of semi-public ownership of the means of production in capitalist society. But just as the tough realities of running a technological society induced the market system to accept and indeed seek larger measures of government intervention, the same realities compel the planned economies to decentralize decisions and rewards. From capitalist thesis and Communist antithesis we may, in good dialectical fashion, be devising a new, working synthesis of the modern industrial society. But if the two versions grow more alike, they also resemble each other in the fact that neither has transcended the *national* market and that the whole apparatus of central decision-making on both sides has reinforced, not weakened, the nation-state. For all the universality of their economic philosophy, the followers neither of Adam Smith nor of Karl Marx have launched mankind so far into an orderly, workable, worldwide version of the technological economy.

The failure of Communist philosophy to deal with the contradictions and dangers of international order should not surprise us. Marx gives us the impression that for him they were all simply rooted in capitalism, private property, and the profit motive. These, he believed, make up the disruptive forces which pit nation against nation. Remove the provocations and envies of an evil, exploitative system and men will live as brothers in a world from which the nation—like the state—will have withered away.

Then the Bolsheviks found themselves in charge of one of the last of the old semi-feudal dinosaur empires, a despotism ruling not only over Russians but over millions of colonial peoples and holding them all together by the old mixture of force and mystical devotion to the emperor. Russia at that time was hardly at the first stage of becoming a large nation-state. It still belonged to an earlier species—Holy Russia, Imperial Russia, Russia that could think of itself as "the third Rome." Any more incongruous capture for a tough-minded crew of modernizing Marxists it is hard to picture, and on the problems raised by state structure or by international relations, their Marxism, as we have remarked, gave them no guidance. If they splashed about a bit in the unfamiliar waters, it is hardly surprising.

Trotsky simply believed no one base could be held for Communism unless the whole world followed suit—a reminder of the universalist side of the Marxist faith. But his attempts to rally Communist revolutions in other states—which included a direct invasion of Poland—came up against other peoples' nationalisms and were so unsuccessful that Lenin finally denounced intervention abroad as the work of "madmen or provocateurs" and said that only revolutions carried through by the people themselves had any hope or value.

Their own Russian colonies they treated, in theory, with the utmost magnanimity. Soon after the Bolshevik take-over, the world had its attention riveted by the announcement of the right of all subject peoples to choose freedom. With Communist governments installed, they "chose" instead to remain inside a federal Soviet Socialist union with their Russian ex-masters. When Georgia inconveniently tried to take the offer of emancipation at its face value, Stalin (a fellow-Georgian) had the land invaded and the idea, not unnaturally, went into eclipse. Similarly, some ten years later, most of the Ukrainian government was liquidated when its distress over collectivization seemed to be stimulating ideas of "bourgeois nationalism."

Within these firmly imposed federal limits, however, Soviet theories of nationalism proved enlightened and even-handed. All the dependent peoples gained by the Communist commitment to education. After a couple of generations there were among the children of Khazak herdsmen a whole new generation of graduate students— a fact which the Bantu herdsmen of South Africa may reflect on wryly when their government promises to defend them against the evils of godless Bolshevism. But it is also true that Russian migrants in considerable numbers have moved into all the Central Asian dependencies and settled there; underneath the forms of federalism, the central government in Moscow has exercised total power. The effect, strongly reinforced by the decision to build socialism in one country, has been to transform the old ramshackle tsarist empire of infinite distances and pieties into a version, a large but increasingly compact version, of the Russian nation-state. Just as the drives of separate nationhood took over the universalist tendencies and aspirations of the descendants of Adam Smith and the Founding Fathers in the United States, the followers of Marx and Lenin underwent the same fate in their Union of Soviet Socialist Republics. Nationalism conquered both the American thesis and the Russian antithesis of the universalist faith. The two great federated experiments, based upon a revolutionary concept of the destiny of all mankind, have ended, in counterpoint, as the two most powerful nation-states in history.

These consolidations occurred before the Second World War but were vastly reinforced by the passions and agonies of the great struggle. Everything that has happened since has helped to confirm the impression of nationalism's driving and undiminished force. It has dissolved the old Western colonial systems and sent fifty new states to the United Nations. It has revived, in spite of direct Soviet occupation, in the Communist states of Eastern Europe. Even the government which seems for the time being most immune to its contagion—the Chinese Peoples' Republic—may well be in the middle of the process virtually completed in Russia, that of turning an old empire into a new nation-state. True, it is still in the first flush of revolution. It still has Trotskyites among its leaders who argue that the revolution itself is not secure until the whole world has been Communized. Revolution is still being exported in the belief that one country can, in spite of Lenin's warning, bring about another's revolution.

But the warning signals already flutter in the revolutionary breeze. First in Malaya and now in Indonesia, the local Communists became too obviously and too unshakably Chinese—Chinese in orientation and loyalty and often Chinese in nationality as well. The revulsion set in—in a long civil war in the Malayan jungles, more suddenly and possibly more speedily among the Indonesian islands—but in both cases sparked by local anti-Chinese nationalism.

At one remove, too many visits by a Chinese Prime Minister to Africa, too many remarks about the continent being "ripe for revolution" strengthened local feeling that Big Brother, however ideologically acceptable, was making his national weight unduly felt and intervening without justification in other nations' business. The Chinese leaders may still be dreaming the universalist dream of a brotherhood of peoples brought about by world-wide Communism. But this is a very early, naïve stage of Communism—before the tough consequences of controlling a territorial base are fully digested, before the particularism of one's own brand of Communism comes up against the particularism of another neighbor with another history and another race. China, confronted with nationalism—the nationalism of non-Communists like Sukarno or of *national* Communists like Kim Il Sung—is basically as nonplused as were the early Soviet leaders. Nationalism should not be there. But it is there. Communism does not act as a dissolvent. On the contrary, by modernizing the economy, increasing literacy, and creating a sense of popular participation, it can even become an agent of national self-consciousness. At first, confronting these paradoxes, the true believer rejects the evidence in favor of the dream. Later, he accommodates himself to it. Russia has virtually reached that stage. The Chinese have not. And this gap in time and resignation makes up one of the bitterest elements in their current, angry, invective-ridden ideological debate.

Does it go further? Does it in fact undermine the whole validity of Communism as an order of explanation and meaning cogent enough and coherent enough to form the philosophical cement of a worldwide order? The non-Marxist would, of course, argue that such is now the case. Marxism's gloomy predictions—of increasing impoverishment, of capitalist immobility, of inevitable imperialism—have been wrong too often to give one much confidence in the "scientific" analysis from which they are derived. Equally Marxism's obstinately hopeful forecasts of diminishing government, of economics solved at the wave of public ownership, of natural harmony between peoples—all seem too naïve to bear the weight of any rational hope about world order.

Apart from some societies in which entrenched feudal remnants or a strong colonial hangover remain, young people seem no longer much interested in Marxism. The wave of the future of the thirties ebbs down the beaches of the world with a sad, diminishing roar.

And it may well be that, outside China, Marxism is in retreat in Communist countries, too. One cause of the Hungarian uprising in 1956 was the government's arrest of students demanding fewer compulsory classes in Marxism. The literature that captivates the young people of Moscow seems to be as near the frontier of unorthodoxy as it is safe to go, and in poetry, beyond it. All through the bloc countries, complaints recur and recur of the indifference and lack of ideological commitment of the young. Between the beatniks of Berkeley and the nonconformists of Moscow University there may well be the bond of weariness with an obsessive orthodoxy—the orthodoxy of bourgeois capitalism and the orthodoxy of bourgeois Communism. These represent the extremes. Yet there is little trace among young people on either side of the ideological divide of Wordsworth's exultation, Adam Smith's cheery hopefulness, or Marx's messianic dream. It is perhaps precisely the vision of automatic progress and rationality that has faded on both sides.

Must we then conclude that mankind's first effort to construct political affinities, a functioning economy, and a system of meaning on a worldwide, post-national scale has proved a failure? In one sense, clearly not. Instinctively, perhaps, but accurately the men of the Enlightenment did perceive what was going to happen to planet Earth. The science and technology which held out such a brilliant promise of future performance have surpassed any dream conceived of their capacity. They have knit the world in a single web of communication. They have given people such access to each other that tourism looks like becoming the biggest industry in the world. They have evolved methods of research and production which enjoy universal validity. They have, almost inconceivably, made the earth itself a launching pad for the voyage to other planets and confronted the human species with new journeys as strange as the journey of the first air-breathing organism out of the primal sea. In a technical, material, physical sense, the unity and universalism of modern global society far outdoes anything the visionaries foresaw. It has become a fact. The failure lies in the human imagination.

So far all efforts to realize that fact in terms of man's political, economic, and moral preoccupations have foundered on his old particularism, his old clannishness, his old nationalism, his old idols of the market and the tribe. "Between the dream and the reality falls the shadow"—but today the reality is not blocking the dream. It is the other way round. The reality is our actual physical planetary present; the dream is all the surviving blocks and pretensions and exclusions of an outdated nationalist past. But the shadow falls just the same—the shadow of nuclear destruction falling across a totally disordered world. To realize a vision only in material power and technical skill and to lose it in ideal and purpose is the ultimate barbarism. This is where we stand today.

Chapter Ten

# The Responsibility
# of Power

**B**UT WE do not have to stay
there. The universalist dream was not mistaken. Indeed
the most powerful and effective forces of our time—our
science and our technology—have realized it. What was
false was to assume that there could be some easy, automatic self-regulating method of achieving the profound
readjustments in political loyalty, economic function,
and philosophical meaning which the new society demands. What is really so curious about both versions of
the liberal society—capitalist or Communist—is how little
thought they give to the hard realities of international

order, how much they assume that inter-state relations will solve themselves and worldwide markets run of their own accord. The capitalist virtually says everything will be all right so long as you keep government out, the Communist if you bring government in. But the amount of sheer hard realistic thought on either side has been minimal, the wash of ideology and feckless optimism phenomenal. It is time for this to stop—on both sides. No *automatic* forces are going to build at the needed, worldwide, level a decent political system, a functioning international economy, or a basis of reconciling and up-lifting purpose. These needs simply have to be moved from the twilight zone of our thinking and given the priority, the urgency, and the attention we give day by day to national interests many of which, because of their international implications, we are virtually power-less to solve single-handed. At least we have to recog-nize where the priorities really lie and give up the as-sumption that some hidden hand will after all pull a rabbit of world order out of our planet's present largely unwearable hat.

Where does realistic thinking begin? Surely in those areas in which relevant concrete achievement is already an historical fact. What men have achieved once, they can achieve again, and orderly political institutions, functioning markets, and sustaining beliefs *have* already organized and vitalized very large areas of the earth's surface supporting very large numbers of the earth's population. If communications no faster than relays of horses and messengers could help to hold together the

Chinese quarter of the human race, supersonic jets and images and voices bounced off space satellites should, technically, do the larger job more easily. True, the vast Chinese empire was a despotism, and this historical route to unity must be counted closed. No *one* center of power will conquer the world into unity. Today conquest means annihilation. We have to plan for a plural world with a number of power centers. In fact, at its appropriate level, the nation, in spite of the fantastic variations in its size and coherence—from 600 thousand people in Gabon to 800 million in China—will almost certainly be a lasting, constituent element in any worldwide supranational system. But it will not be an ultimate element. After all, we are used to diffuse loyalties. A sense of the clan survives in Scotland. The sense of being Scottish survives in Britain. The sense of being British is very likely to survive in a European Union. So will the sense of being French. Anyone who knows France finds incomprehensible the fear that such a land could in any real sense be submerged. It is far more likely to give all its neighbors, like its Africans, a Gallic tinge. And Europe in turn will have a sense of itself in any intercontinental association. No unity in the world will make Latin and "Anglo-Saxon" America alike. Anyway, who wants them to be? A world of interchangeable men and women is precisely the Orwellian nightmare of 1984.

The issue is function, not standardization. It is a sound principle of human order that social tasks should be left at the simplest and most human level at which they can be adequately performed—beginning with the family.

Everyone understands the sense of a hierarchy of responsibility *inside* the nation. The central government does not overlay, just for the fun of it, the responsibilities that can best be carried by cities and counties or, in a federation, by the constituent states. But owing to the fixation of men's minds on *national* sovereignty, the top of the world's political pyramid is not there. We recognize authority and hierarchy up through all the levels of political, economic, and social need. Then, when at the highest level we reach the ultimate issues of survival itself, we recognize none. There is simply a blank arena, filled with the pressures and counter-pressures of irresponsible power. No one can call this reason. It represents a total failure of imagination and rationality.

It is not even as though the powers which would have, of necessity, to be exercised at a world level need be very extensive. Over much of the earth's surface federations as large as the United States or the Soviet Union have resources and scope enough to meet most of their citizens' needs and satisfy most of their aspirations. If similar federal structures could be established in other continents—Europe, Africa, Latin America, the Indian sub-continent—the underpinning of world order at subsidiary levels would be much more stable. Nor is this an entirely empty hope. Today, with some genuine enthusiasm and also with the hypocritical tribute vice pays to virtue, movements have started in most of these areas to edge toward greater unity, even if elderly and flamboyant anachronisms like General de Gaulle stand in the way.

At the world level, the political task lies almost solely in preventing war. Of course this fact also makes the range of tasks the most difficult, the most sensitive, the most frenzied of all for here national pride, illusions of grandeur, the pretensions of prestige, and all the paranoid follies of which man is capable rush to the protection of interests which may in themselves be perfectly legitimate but which can be neither realized nor mediated in the middle of the surrounding hysteria.

Yet within states methods of dealing with the most passionate conflicts of interest have been worked out. The rule of law, protected by an impartial police force and exercised through law courts, through rules of equity, through mediation, conciliation, and arbitration has brought the violent self-assertion of individual citizens, of groups, corporations, and subsidiary authorities under reasonable control. General Motors, whose corporate income is larger than that of a quarter of the world's nation-states, does not thunder "My interests, right or wrong" and hire thugs to settle the matter by violence. For all its power, its imagination is tamed by the acceptance of the need for legal settlement. Governments could be as peace-loving—and indeed as prosperous—were it not for the disastrous conviction loose in the world that the hierarchy of responsibility ends at the level of national sovereignty. Below may be law. All above is force.

Admittedly, we have made a first timid step toward the acceptance of worldwide law. The United Nations exists above all to provide alternatives to violence. Its meetings and corridors provide the informal venue for national leaders in search of compromise. Its debates attempt to build up a world consensus with enough moral force to deter aggressors. On a few occasions it has actually been able to act in a full governmental fashion—imposing solutions, as in the Katanga, or policing areas of danger, in Cyprus, in the Gaza Strip, along the cease-fire line in Kashmir. These are not negligible achievements. If its intervention could be extended to such areas as Southeast Asia, the use of purely American power to deter Chinese "adventurism" could be withdrawn. If our eyes were not all but blinded by nationalist myopia, we would see in both the achievements and the possible extensions of the United Nations police power the most hopeful growing points of a world in which nuclear annihilation could cease to be, as it is now, a near-certainty.

But the United Nations is still no more than a mock-version of the kind of central power the world needs if it is to survive. Great states retain all but absolute sovereignty through the veto. All states tend to see the organization as a forum for maneuver and pressure on others rather than as an august symbol of the authority all accept. Nor will much difference be made by changes, however rational and desirable, in its machinery. Weighted voting, majority decisions, the abolition of the veto all no doubt make sense in rational terms, but they amount to very little unless a profound change occurs in the attitudes of the governments themselves. A Great Power does not cease to be a Great Power if the veto goes. Its simple scale of might is a veto since no outside force can exercise coercion without unleashing total war. The change has to come from a conversion, a new realism, a rational conviction that once the bomb is invented, only a world with peaceful means of settling disputes has any hope of avoiding ultimate incineration. And as every drunk, every addict, every paranoid will tell you, many prefer the disease to the cure.

It is for this reason that, at this stage of human development, a special responsibility seems to lie on the greatest Power in history, the United States. It is, in some ways, the least trammeled with age-long memories of separate grandeur. It came to birth and then it came of age in a world already tilted toward universal solutions. It has kept, under its Americanism, a wider sense of the family of man. For this reason alone, American vision and American prodding helped to create whatever international institutions now exist. Moreover, America is already in a sense a plural world. It has had to absorb the nationalities of the world. It struggles bravely with the more difficult task of absorbing the races, too. It knows that diversity will remain the rule of any human society and in its complex but open federal system, it has given pluralism a working political form.

The degree to which this inheritance fits the United States to pioneer the new tasks of world order can best be illustrated by comparing with it the other great federal community of the modern age—Soviet Russia. There both history and ideology have so far reinforced the

closed society. Tsarist Russia never made the break to
liberal institutions, and the Marxist illusion that the state
would wither away—which would doubtless have been
proved an illusion anywhere—came straight up against
one of the oldest, toughest, most encrusted traditions of
holy despotism in the world. To expect such a state to
take a lead in building the institutions of an open world
would be to strain hopefulness too far. The miracle is
that the monolith will sit down in the United Nations'
plural community, put itself in a position to be judged
by its neighbors, dourly defend itself, when outnum-
bered, with the veto, and on occasion even participate
in a vote, a policy, or a decision. Statesmen from open
societies tend to forget how extraordinary it is that Russia participates at all. Some of the liberal and universalist content of Marxism has after all survived in the
despotic Russian container. The language of freedom
and popular democracy—like the mask of virtue—may
begin as hypocrisy. It could end as truth—whereas there
is no "give" in the language of blood and soil and
frenzied national paranoia. Hitler's reaction to the plural
society of the League of Nations was to march Germany
out.

Nonetheless the world of voting, of lobbying, of open
decisions openly arrived at is not Russia's present, natural, comfortable environment. The lead in pushing,
prodding, persuading, and guiding the nations toward
the acceptance of minimal but essential world authority
in the cause of peace can come only from the United
States. True, it should be supported by every democ-

racy with a comparable tradition of the open society. Nowhere perhaps does General de Gaulle's reactionary nationalism show itself more ominously than in his readiness to compete with Russia in limiting even the most modest extensions of United Nations responsibility.

And few contemporary hardenings of the nationalist position are more tragic than that of India in its dispute with Pakistan. If the nation of Ashoka, Gandhi, and Nehru, if the great plural democracy of Asia cannot find ways to mediate a solution on the basis of the generosity, conciliation, and peaceful settlement it successfully and rightly claimed and exercised in 1947, then the ultimate chances of the rule of law, not force, in Asia seem remote indeed. India could be, as it were, as much the democratic pole of the vast Asian community as the United States has become in the Western world. But if self-righteous nationalism takes over and reliance on force becomes the rule, it is difficult to see victory in Asia for any but the most powerful community—which will be not the Indians but the Chinese.

There is a further reason for America's primacy in the tasks of peace. Peace does not consist only in the absence of conflict. It also entails some abatement in the causes of conflict. In fact, one can argue that if a man gives up his "right" to settle his grievances by private force, he may reasonably ask his government to see that they do not become too intolerable. The societies where civil peace reigns are not on the whole the most neglected, the most poverty-stricken, the most disillusioned. Violence breaks out in Watts, not Westchester County.

The whole world has now passed beyond the phase of ignorant, passive, resigned destitution. Propaganda and communication have seen to it that everywhere, in Adlai Stevenson's celebrated phrase, the "revolution of rising expectations" works like a leaven. And in this worldwide society, the contrast between Watts and Westchester does not seem too far-fetched.

In 1965, the combined incomes of the white wealthy post-colonial North Atlantic nations who make up some twenty per cent of the world's peoples, passed the million million dollar mark—which is about seventy per cent of the world's income. Latin America subsists on an annual income of $60 billion—a sum the United States *adds* to its income in eighteen months. Africa's income is half as small again. These are the contrasts. Put into concrete terms, they mean half the expectation of life, five or six times the infant mortality, a fraction of the literacy, diets without protein, rural slums without work, city slums without drains or water. The gap between the nations to the North of the Tropic of Cancer and the rest of the world is fully as wide as the gap between nineteenth-century tycoons and the raw, bewildered migrants huddling on Ellis Island.

Yet the gap, domestically, has been diminished. Larger shares in the national wealth through higher wages and "fringe benefits," transfers from rich to poor by taxation to increase education, health, and skills— these measures have transformed the migrants into citizens and turned the masses into the vast consuming market of the modern economy.

In the international economy, measures to give the developing continents more steady prices for their exports and to open up Western markets to their goods would, in a similar way, increase the "wages" they earn for their services in the world market. And sustained technical and capital assistance, increasing skills and health, providing infrastructure and building up the technological base of the modern economy would, like taxation at home, help to create peoples better able to help themselves.

All this we know. We have accurate estimates from such impartial bodies as the World Bank to show that at this moment, the poor nations could absorb roughly another four billion dollars a year in constructive investment. But ever since the flow of Western capital reached nine billion in 1961, there it has stuck. Meanwhile Western income has grown by another $150 billion. The proportion of aid to national income is, therefore, falling while expectations continue to rise.

In all this the United States occupies a special position. It accounts for three quarters of the increase in Atlantic income and it started the sixties from a national income base of nearly $600 billion. If it set the precedent of devoting to aid one per cent of income, the sum would still only represent a quarter of its *annual* growth in wealth. In short, the sum itself would not be noticed. The burdens are political, not economic. Disappointments go all the way from Kashmir to Latin America's propensity for inflation. At home, they include "a weariness with well doing" that fails to produce immediate and spectacular results. So, at the moment, the wealthiest people in human history appear to be in a phase of disillusion about the consequences of generosity. Just so did Victorian duchesses speak of the "bad poor" who put coals in the bath. And if there is no drive in America to put life, drive, and enthusiasm back into the concept of international aid, no other nation is likely to shoulder the task.

At a factual level, the arguments against this attitude can only be made country by country, case by case. There are hundreds of success stories to set against the grisly examples of failure. How many people, for instance, know of the help given by the World Bank and the British Government to transform the long contested "White Highlands" in Kenya into an area of settled African farming? How many people know that the controversial Volta hydroelectric scheme was completed a year ahead of time and at a cost of $15 million less than the contract price? Who knows that in the rear of the Vietnam fighting, the first dams of the Mekong River scheme have actually been built? Who knows about Pakistan's agricultural breakthrough on the basis of tube wells? Of Central America's successful experiment in a common market? Of Africa's fantastic drive for education? Of the recent ending of aid to Taiwan and Greece? Of Mexico's surge to modernity? The failures hit the headlines. The successes are regarded as routine.

If anyone had looked at the British economy between 1800 and 1850—as it looked to Dickens or the "dismal scientists"—he might well have concluded that the whole experiment was destined to fail. The developing "South" is similarly entering on the fifty-year cycle of "break-through" to modernity. The first stages always look a mess. But it is unreasonable, it is folly to condemn on ten years' evidence an experiment which must, of necessity, take four or five decades to complete.

Today the issue is above all one of keeping faith. Better shares and progressive taxation helped to raise up the poor and create the modern market *inside* domestic society. We have to believe that similar policies, conducted as steadily, will have the same economic effect in the world at large—and will in addition profoundly influence political attitudes by ending the picture of wealthy white colonialists exploiting the "helpless" peoples of the developing world. Such a change is not a matter of policy or machinery. These are largely available. The World Bank, the International Development Authority, the International Monetary Fund, the United Nations Special Fund—all these organizations contain enough skilled and experienced men to run the economic organs of a world authority. The sums involved are relatively puny—some $12 billion a year compared with the $120 billion the developed world, capitalist and Communist together, spend on a system of armed security which threatens them both with extinction. Even as an insurance, it is not expensive. As the only means available to counter the grievances which lead to war, it looks positively cheap.

But it has little appeal. It inspires little enthusiasm

and devotion. And the reason is simple. It lies in that lifeless zone beyond the thoughts of national voters and beyond the direct responsibility of national governments. Policies which are reasonable for Appalachia or Tyneside stop dead at the seashore. The reasons have nothing to do with culture or economic necessity or facts of any kind. They are simply rooted in the nonworking of human imagination, responsibility, and generosity once the blinkers of nationalism go on. Today faith, not fact, is what cripples our programs, closes our pockets, and dries up our hearts.

Chapter Eleven

# A Sense of Humanity

C AN THERE be a change
of faith? Here we reach the third of our categories of
human order—the order of meaning and purpose in
human life. Clearly it is not only the hopes of automatic
political peace and self-functioning markets on a worldwide scale that have faded from the vision of our world
inherited from the Enlightenment. All our ideological
ancestors—British Puritans, Founding Fathers, French
revolutionaries, even the Marxists and Leninists—have
centered their faith on the dignity of man and his ability
to build the human city. Yet man has remained obstinately "tribal" and has used the instruments that were
to liberate him to maim and destroy fellowmen wearing

( 118 )

another label. He has even produced a society which, openly and as a matter of principle, did what others have done only under cover of excuses or "provocations." Hitler established a state on the basis of the Germans' innate superiority to other peoples and killed six million Jews to prove the point. Not often in history has the essential dignity of man been turned into such mockery as at Auschwitz or Maidenek. The age of the religion of man produced his most agonizing martyrdom.

What went wrong? Not surely the ideal itself. If man is not worthy of dignity and respect, what is? If man is not to aim at building a decent human order, at what shall he aim? If the vision of the Enlightenment—of man free, responsible, fraternal, equal in standing and op- portunity—is not a worthy vision, then there *are* no worthy visions on earth. The difficulty cannot be said to lie in the philosophy. It must lie in its failure to take hold of human hearts and to exorcize the older, deeper, more primitive and existential emotions of separate, hos- tile, tribal communities surviving only at each other's expense.

We have therefore to look not so much at the philoso- phy as at its roots and sanctions. It is, of course, an historical fact that the vision of man as the crown of evolutionary creation and as a significant and respon- sible co-worker in the construction of a creative human order is a profoundly religious vision mediated to the world from Hellenic and Jewish sources by way of Western Christianity. Man's value and dignity spring from the metaphysical equality of all souls in the sight

( 119 )

of their Creator. His creativeness is derived from a God who has, in some inconceivable fashion, handed over an unfinished universe to His creature and offered him the choice of helping—or not—to build the heavenly city.

Yet obviously one can look at man from many other angles of vision—as the fittest to survive, as a biological sport, as a momentary leaf on the tree of life, as a "forked radish," as a cosmic bad joke, as a meaningless collection of molecules differing in energy but not significance from other molecular lumps. It takes very little expertise to prove that he is a creature of his chemistry or his drives or his environment or of the number of times he was dropped in the nursery. Proof of his dignity and freedom seems to escape the laboratory tests. In fact, objective examination suggests varieties so vast in capacity, intelligence, energy—let alone attractiveness—that they point not so much to equality and fair shares and dignity as to a hierarchy of men with talent at the top and helots at the bottom. It takes really lively faith to look at a cinema queue on a wet November afternoon and still believe in man's dignity and ability to build the Great Society.

We have then to accept that our vision of man is a vision of faith and that the two great versions of the faith in the modern world—Liberal and Marxist—have not conquered particularism, have not conquered tribalism, have not freed us from nationalism, in short, have not yet taught us to be human. So, in a sense, while keeping the vision, we have to begin all over again to

find less facile, automatic, and utopian grounds for believing it.

For some, the new roots will lie in a renewed sense
of the validity of the Christian or Jewish vision. Others
will say that they offer no route back. Christianity is
the system of meaning evolved over a particular time
in the specific society of Western Europe. Jewry is even
more limited—the faith, however astonishing, of a tiny
tribe. But no one can now talk of going "back" to the
old faiths. They are no longer there to go back to. The
traditional faiths of the West—whose secular versions
have more or less conquered but not united the world—
are undergoing a revolution so surprising and so far-
reaching that out of it could well emerge a new encounter between faith in man and religious faith.

Two aspects of this religious revolution can profoundly affect the encounter. One is the reaching out to
all the other formulations of man's worth and destiny
and the attempt to discover in them the basis for dia-
logue, for respect, for an alliance, if you like, against
existential despair. Christianity which drove round the
world as the white man's faith, knocking down the idols
and converting the heathen, is beginning a new, more
discreet and modest journey to find out what lay behind "the idols" it so confidently demolished, only to let
in frenzied nationalism and secularized ideologies
through the empty shrines. Since Catholicism has been
by far the most historically rooted and culturally de-
fined of Europe's faiths, the new approach seems most
remarkable when it comes from the Vatican Council

in an all but unanimous affirmation of the bishops of the Church that they must seek and love the purity of Buddhist asceticism, the mystical sense of the Hindus, the dedicated monotheism of the Moslems, the vision of God the Father and Creator shared by Jews and Christians in the stupendous images of the Old Testament; more, that they must find and respect the compassion for man and the devotion to his service among many who would call themselves non-believers, humanists, Marxists, even atheists in the strictest sense.

We cannot tell what will follow from so new a voyage of discovery. But it at least contains the possibility that all round the world the views of life which have tried, in Paul Tillich's phrase, to give man a "dimension of depth" may be found to possess in common (and hence strengthen and enhance) some profound insights into human predicaments and hopes. That pride and self-love blind a man to his neighbors' needs, all have taught. That no moral rule can stand unless a man concedes to another what he demands for himself is the commonplace of all religious thinking. That love is a disciplined readiness to seek another's good—not emotion, not possessiveness—is also commonly taught. Most religions see a living link between the depths of man's being and the ground of all existence—however expressed. And all, even the secular Confucians, have believed, ever since the great moral revolution in the millennia before Christ, that the ultimate law of man's being is a moral law, reflecting a larger harmony in the whole universe—a harmony the Chinese described as "the way of heaven" and Dante as "the love that moves the sun and the other stars."

If these are the common insights into man's "dimension of depth," then clearly every one of them directly contradicts the basic instinct of nationalism—that *my* kind of man is special and every other kind of man is not. Every one of them depends for its validity on the fact of a humanity, a dignity, and a value common to *all* mankind. It is, therefore, possible that the new journey of discovery made by religious men may uncover a new opposition to frantic tribalism and give a sense of rootedness to the vision of human dignity and human freedom that no utopian ideology could hope to provide.

The other aspect of the revolution may not be new but today it seems to be gathering momentum. It is an attempt not simply to map and define the "dimension of depth" but to discover it and live in it. Beyond the barriers of class and creed and race and nation there live our fellowmen—not dummies, not abstractions, not enemies, but living breathing men who are neighbors, men in want, in confusion, men in anger and rejection, men to whom their fellows must reach out, men with whom they must discover not in theory but in practice what it is to share this human substance. Young people off to the Peace Corps, worker priests in the slums of Paris, young Komsomols volunteering for schools in the Arctic, nuns in Calcutta giving starving beggars off the streets the privilege of a decent death—the examples are worldwide. They make up pockets of a new elite who are so far beyond our angry nationalisms that, like the just men of the Talmudic legend, their profound humanity may well hold up the rooftrees of heaven for all mankind.

And for many people today one figure comes to mind in this company of renewers and reconcilers—a very old man who on the very edge of death brought back to one of the world's most venerable and encrusted institutions the seeds of a springlike revival. In Pope John, the sense of our common humanity reached, if you like, a point of genius. He was not a "father-figure." He was the true image of paternal love and perhaps no words can better give his sense of the unity and reality of all human relations than his farewell words to Khrushchev's daughter and her husband, the Adjubheis. "They tell me," he said, "that you are atheists. But you will not refuse the blessing of an old man for your children." And, at this point, so we hear, they knelt down and wept.

The fact that faith in man can find deeper resources than secular ideology does not, of course, mean that mankind will seek them out. Indeed, as we stand on this strange, threatened world that overlooks Armageddon, we cannot be sure that any of our needs—for political cooperation, for economic generosity, for faith in man— will be realized or rather will be realized in time. The lessons "of our proud and angry dust" are hard to learn, the temptations of arrogance and separateness and self-assertion all but irresistible. Yet once before after eons of external magic, of manipulation and propitiatory sacrifice, men did turn from the legion of idols to worship the central Good and to discover their own nature "in spirit and i.. truth." It is just possible that we, too, have been bemused by the magic of our vast technology and by the incantations of our ideology and have thought to remake the earth by means as automatic as the click of a prayer wheel or the burning of a goat. But it does not seem that the reality we live in can be changed by such externals. It is only within the context of a deeper faith that we shall discover the love and fortitude we need to build a reconciled and peaceful society for man.